10 Perils in Parish Ministry And How to Handle Them

The Pastor's Survival Manual

Kenneth Alan Moe

An Alban Institute Publication

The Publication Program of The Alban Institute is assisted by a grant from Trinity Church, New York City.

Library of Congress Catalog Card Number 95-78603
ISBN #1-56699-157-9

CONTENTS

FOREWORD

Effective clergy sustain their growing edge. They continue to face into the places where they are frightened and confused. It is here that they find their most profound growing edge. This is where effectiveness in ministry requires both courage and persistence. When we consistently attack all these frightening and confusing aspects in our personal life, as well as in our role as resident religious authority, we break through to new levels of wholeness that are the foundation of effective ministry.

Whether we like it or not, we as clergy are in the health and wholeness business. We are among the few generalists left in society. When other professionals are able to branch out into specialities, the local parish pastor needs to be good at a variety of roles and tasks. Our profession is one of the few that still deal with the total person, physically, emotionally, mentally, and spiritually. When people are physically ill, we visit them in hospitals and nursing homes and we pray for them, possibly engaging in the ancient ritual of laying on of hands. When people are emotionally off balance, we attend to them as well, engaging in pastoral counseling. When people are off base intellectually, we preach to those issues or provide learning opportunities for them. The spiritual ill health of our people and society demands our unending vigilance. And we as generalists are going to be effective in addressing this total ministry in direct proportion to our own health and wholeness—physically, emotionally, mentally, and spiritually. Anything we do to move us into greater health on any one of these levels is going to make us more effective as professionals in ministry. When we speak we will be more credible because we exemplify our message more completely. When people meet us they tend to listen to what we say because our personhood manifests what we speak.

We forget we make a profound theological statement the moment we set foot inside a room, even before we open our mouth. People take one look at us and decide whether we have anything to offer them. Our total health, or lack of it, is hanging out in public view. When we lack balance in life or a healthy disposition, people wonder why the Gospel we preach doesn't seem to work for us. "Physician heal thyself" is what they want to say to us.

It is precisely at this point that Ken Moe's book enters as another useful tool in this quest for wholeness and effectiveness in ministry. Reading this book is like taking a survey on how well you are managing to avoid these ten perils. Falling prey to these perils not only diminishes your effectiveness as a pastor, it also takes a chunk out of your soul, and when you are not hitting on all cylinders in your personal life, you will be less competent in your ministry. The first step to remedy this is not to learn additional skills, but to get your personal life back in balance and then approach your ministry in an alternative fashion.

I believe this to the bottom of my socks. Our job as religious professionals is to take on—one at the time—our addictions, our neurotic patterns, our fears and anxieties, our self-defeating personality traits, our physically destructive lifestyles, our hang-ups, and continually pursue our journey into wholeness and balance. As we grow older and experience the effects of aging—loss of some aspect of stamina and health—we can still become healthier, and every victory in overcoming anything that detracts from total health makes us more credible and effective in our ministry. Ken Moe's book is a good tool in this journey toward wholeness.

I am especially impressed with Moe's sense of the order of importance of the ten perils. The higher the number the more important he feels the peril is. Given the panic that judicatory officials are in related to clergy sexual malfeasance, you would expect the author to list sexual addiction as number ten. Yet addictions and co-dependence are listed as traps seven and eight. I believe he's got it right. The top reason why clergy don't succeed in parish ministry is conditional love. One of the key reasons congregations fire their ministers is because, at root, they feel the ministers really don't like them. They find it hard to say this outright so they begin to find faults with other parts of the ministry, such as sermons, work routines, calling, being available to people, etc.

Once again, I do not believe this is merely a matter of taste, but has more to do with the unintegrated part of the clergyperson's shadow, which rather than being owned gets projected onto congregants. These clergy are finding faults in their congregants that they have not really owned up to within their own psyche. It is a part of their lack of emotional wholeness.

In any case, I am excited you have picked up this book. I hope you will venture more deeply into it. In some very practical ways, Moe brings great depth of wisdom in his admonitions to us clergy. In doing so he gives us a glimpse of the things we can do to better prepare us to meet the spiritual hunger of our people. The church at large is going to be healthier because of his work.

Roy Oswald

ACKNOWLEDGMENTS

Writing a book is a cooperative enterprise. The notion that a book is the product of an author working alone in some quiet hideaway is not accurate. Regardless of where the author writes, many people are involved in transforming a series of ideas into a book. The people named below have played significant roles in the creation of *The Pastor's Survival Manual*.

I am grateful to my colleague in ministry, Elder Carolyn B. Stephens, Executive Presbyter of the Indian Nations Presbytery in Oklahoma, and to my friend, Dr. Jake Thiessen of Mechanicsburg, Pennsylvania, to my wife, the Reverend Shelly Moe, pastor of the Presbyterian Congregation of Middletown, Pennsylvania, for their editorial comments and critical evaluations of the manuscript in progress. I have incorporated suggestions from each of them into the present text, providing much improvement. Alban Editor Celia Allison Hahn deserves praise for her editorial wisdom and for her keen but kind way of identifying my many textual intuitive leaps. Copy editor Dimples Kellogg helped, too, paring my wordy sentences and activating my passive verbs. And I thank the Reverend Herbert L. Bomberger, Director of the Bethany Counseling Ministry (United Church of Christ) of Harrisburg, Pennsylvania, for his productive insights and encouraging words.

One more acknowledgment is due. When the outmoded computer I used to write this book proved to be incompatible with The Alban Institute's system, my daughter, Cedar Kennan, came to the rescue with her much more up-to-date equipment. Thanks, Cedar. I plan to invest my royalties in a new computer, so by buying this book the reader will be contributing toward upgrading the author. This seems to me like a good thing for a reader to do. I hope you think so, too.

This work is dedicated to two of my guiding stars: in praise, to Erasmus, and in love, to Shelly.

Providet Deus.

The Wilderness

This epigram he added thereunto,
That if gold rust, what then shall iron do?
For if the parson's base, in whom we trust,
No wonder that the layfolk turn to rust.[1]

So wrote Geoffrey Chaucer about that parson in the prologue to his
Canterbury Tales. This book is about Chaucer's parson and countless
others who give their lives to parish ministry. Whether they are called
ministers, priests, preachers, pastors, parsons, rectors, or any number of
other names and titles, people who serve congregations labor on the front
lines of their religious traditions. Parish ministry requires talent and
abilities that are rare in the general population, and in this present age
of specialization, it may be the only major profession left that requires
the skills of a generalist. Because of this rarity, Geoffrey Chaucer's
metaphor of gold to represent the pastor is apt. Other associations come
to mind as well. Gold is a symbol of commitment in relationships. It is
also malleable, not brittle, so it can be formed into shapes highly valued
by the people. Historically, gold has been discovered, mined, and even
refined in the wilderness. Through personal and ecclesiastical experiences, pastors can resonate with all of these metaphorical dimensions of
this esteemed element.

There are, of course, many other kinds of ministry. Women and
men are called to be chaplains, pastoral counselors, religious educators,
denominational officials, comtemplatives, spiritual directors, and more.
In the larger context, people are called by God to ministry as social
workers, carpenters, nurses, administrators, and grocery clerks. But this

book focuses on the peculiar world of parish ministry and the problems inherent in that world. For reasons of simplicity I have chosen the word *pastor* to stand for any of the other words commonly understood to mean the person who is the spiritual leader of a congregation.

The couplets from the *Canterbury Tales* quoted above identify the pastor (parson) as gold and the laypeople as iron. This should not be taken to mean, however, that pastors are inherently more precious than parishioners. To extend Chaucer's metaphor, if some parishioners are iron, certainly others are platinum, lead, tin, and even uranium. To be worthy of the metaphor, pastors must bear responsibly the attributes of gold and relate faithfully to all the other elements in their congregations.

Perhaps, after reading this book, some pastors may want to reconsider their calls to ministry and think about other forms of service rather than remain in the parish. Some who are now in seminary may be tempted to change direction away from the parish and toward different kinds of ministry. My hope is that most pastors will find within these pages some helpful ways to strengthen their ministries.

Twenty-five years of clergy watching and a half a dozen years of serving as a pastor to pastors have taught me that more often than not, pastors get in trouble with their congregations. Untroubled pastor-parish relationships are the exception rather than the rule. The causes of this phenomenon are legion, arising out of the unrestricted abilities of pastors, families of pastors, and parishioners to create ingenious impediments to effective ministry. That is why I have written this book.

The source of the problem in any particular situation may be the pastor, members of the pastor's family, one or more parishioners, or the culture of the congregation or community. Thus, the pastor may or may not have direct control over the problem. But in every case the pastor carries responsibility for dealing with the problem as well as the capacity to make it much worse.

The following chapters present what I have come to see as the most common problems that jeopardize pastoral ministry. In general, the chapters progress from less difficult to more difficult matters, especially as they concern the long-term harmful effects on pastors, although every chapter deals with serious subjects.

The research supporting this book was gathered inductively from my wide-ranging interactions with hundreds of pastors and not from controlled sociological surveys. Conversations with colleagues in other governing bodies and denominations are reflected in the examples and descriptions provided. Prior to becoming a pastor to pastors, I served in parish ministry in small town, suburban, and city settings and in both solo and multiple staff positions. Therefore, ruminations on my own experiences also appear in these pages.

"We have as many grammars and grammarians," Desiderius Erasmus notes in *The Praise of Folly*.[2] This work represents my peculiar grammar of ministry, subject to the limitations of my knowledge and experience and affected by my tendency to make intuitive leaps. Therefore, I will accept cheerfully any criticism and humbly any praise that comes from readers with their different grammars. My hope is that all the idioms and metaphors are clear and that all examples are fairly given. "But," again I quote from *Folly*, "it is not my business to sift too narrowly the lives of prelates and priests for fear I seem to have intended rather a satire than an oration, and be thought to tax good princes while I praise the bad."[3] Nothing here has been written with malice in mind, but some of my words have arisen from frustratingly painful situations, while other words have come to the page out of foolish events.

All the factors described here represent multiple occurrences I have observed among pastors, and some of these things I have recognized in myself. I have included only phenomena I have encountered repeatedly in numbers of people. Although it is theoretically possible that one pastor could fall into all of these traps, I have never met anyone who has achieved that dubious distinction. Looking at the list from another perspective, however, I can also say that I have never met anyone who has experienced only one. Where one of these occurs, others are likely to figure in as well. Thus, these subjects are not distinctly separated but are interwoven in many patterns in the fabric of parish ministry. Consequently, certain comments are repeated in varying contexts in different chapters of the book to demonstrate the interrelatedness of the subjects.

When I was in college, a good friend took me along on a visit to a Franciscan retreat center near Phoenix. Jeff wanted to see a priest who had been very helpful to him when he was younger. The priest was in town to lead a retreat for fourteen-year-old boys.

As we walked into the room, the priest was tinkering with a wooden box with a slot in the top—an old-fashioned ballot box. He told us that he would be talking to the boys about sex, and until a few minutes earlier, the box had been in the lobby so the boys could write anonymously and put in the box any questions they had about this sensitive subject. The priest would pull the questions out and answer them later that day.

He went on to explain that very few questions had been put in the box, and those were innocuous ones. "They are afraid to ask about— even anonymously—what they really want to know," the priest said, "so I stuff the box with my own provocative questions about the things that are on the minds of adolescent boys."

I suggested that as he read aloud his own material, the boys would be glancing around the room, wondering who had the guts to ask *those* questions.

"Yes," he responded, "but I never have to worry about keeping their attention."

This book follows the lead of that Franciscan priest by presenting some questions and issues that pastors have been afraid to raise publicly. I know from daily experience that the concerns addressed in the chapters that follow are on the minds of many church folk—pastors, parishioners, seminarians, and denominational officials—and they need to be talked about openly. If I have stuffed this book with provocative material, my intent is not to sensationalize in order to keep the reader's attention but to deal honestly with the significant problems that threaten the health and lives of people who serve in parish ministry.

My role as pastor to pastors is still relatively rare in North American denominational life, but the field in growing. I work on the staff of a regional governing body (a presbytery) of the Presbyterian Church (USA). My primary responsibility is to provide pastoral care and counseling for all clergy and their families in our presbytery. In this capacity I stand beside the leadership structure rather than within it in order to maintain appropriate levels of confidentiality and to be in a position to mediate between pastors and governing bodies of the Church. One way confiden- tiality is reinforced is the firm policy that I not serve as a reference for any pastor seeking a new call. Since there are at present so few pastors to pastors, I have been approached for care and counsel by pastors from other presbyteries and other denominations, also, and I have sought to accommodate them to whatever extent seemed appropriate.

Entering into parish ministry is often like entering into a wilderness. Whether it be tangled undergrowth or unforgiving desert, pastors are put to the test by what they encounter in the wilderness. They need inner strength and courage to meet the challenges they encounter. Wit and wisdom are essential, and patience and grace are tools that they must not leave behind.

The next ten chapters explore the wilderness and identify the things that impede pastoral journeys, hamper effective ministry, and destroy spiritual growth primarily in pastors but also in congregations. The afterword enlarges the context to include candidates for ministry—the pastors of the twenty-first century—and examines the woundedness among pastors of all generations. If any reader finds the numbered chapters discouraging, the afterword ends with notes of encouragement and hope.

CHAPTER 1

Poor Education

Ideally, all pastors are well: well-educated, well-read, well-informed, well-rounded. Pastors are expected to be interested in a wide variety of topics, able to converse with just about anybody about nearly anything. Not only does the pastor fill the role of resident sage, but also is often sought out as the fount of reliable facts about life. Wisdom and knowledge are the tools of the ministerial trade.

Whether or not these expectations are fair, it is fair to say that pastors who are not well-educated do not do well. Poor education among clergy is manifested in a number of ways. Even among the traditions that require extensive education prior to ordination, poorly educated pastors manage to slip through the gates and meander through the glebes of the church.

Perhaps the place to look first is the undergraduate college curriculum. The current debate over the value of the traditional liberal arts curriculum in colleges is pertinent to the matter of clergy education. Some argue that a classical liberal arts education is no longer relevant or useful. Technical education and early specialization are needed to meet the needs of the twenty-first century, they say. What happened in ancient Greece, nineteenth-century English novels and poetry, the work of Renaissance painters, the ideas of Enlightenment philosophers, and the dynamics that created World War I are not worth studying, according to this argument.

This is not the place to argue the case for liberal arts education for everyone, but for those who would become pastors, the absence of a broad liberal arts education is a handicap to effective ministry. Seminary curriculums are built on the assumption that seminarians have had prior education in languages, history, science, philosophy, and the fine arts, as well as exposure to the religious traditions of their respective denominations.

Seminary professors expect a great deal of liberal arts lore to be common knowledge among their students. For this reason, seminarians who have undergraduate degrees in such fields as business, engineering, and even education may find themselves distinctly disadvantaged in the classroom unless they have absorbed this kind of information on their own. A seminarian with a degree in engineering who is a history buff, therefore, has an edge over a classmate with a similar degree whose hobby is assembling electronic components.

Beyond seminary, the lack of broadly based knowledge may show up in everything from sermon preparation to day-to-day conversations with parishioners. This does not mean that pastors without liberal arts educations cannot do well. Another factor in poor education is lack of comprehensive reading. Regardless of the extent or quality of undergraduate or seminary education, pastors who read continuously over a wide range of subjects do better than those who do not.

Too narrow an education can jeopardize effective ministry, and too shallow an education can do likewise. Some part of a pastor's training must include in-depth study. Typically, the area where a pastor can achieve deep mastery is the field of religion (theology, knowledge of scripture, church history, etc.), and this is doubly fitting, for it can enrich the pastor's teaching role with the congregation and bring the pastor an added sense of confidence.

All this may sound like a call for clerical elitism through intellectual achievement, but it is not. Pastors must not claim positions of superiority by cloaking themselves in academic robes. They must speak plainly with parishioners and avoid talking down to anyone. They must translate theological jargon into words their parishioners can understand. They must communicate through the idioms of the people, including those derived from popular culture, such as movies, television, and sports. Having done this, however, pastors remain representatives of universal wisdom and bearers of Church lore for their congregations, so in that context they need to know their business. Unsophisticated parishioners are capable of asking complex theological questions, and the well-educated pastor is ready for the test and willing to answer thoughtfully.

Continuing Education

The area of education most neglected by pastors is continuing education. Many denominations require or at least encourage pastors to continue their studies through seminars, extra course work, certification training, current reading, and other events. Frequently, congregations provide allowances to cover the costs of events and books. Yet many pastors fail to take advantage of these opportunities and let the allowances lapse rather that keep current in their educations.

One excuse commonly given, especially by pastors of small congregations, is that they wish to save their congregations a little money by not using their continuing education accounts. But the effect is to short-change congregations by depriving them of the educational refreshment that would help their pastors serve them better. Deferred maintenance of the physical plant of a church eventually results in great costs that cannot be avoided. The same applies to deferred continuing education. It eventually catches up with a pastor, who, like an aging boiler, needs to be replaced.

Occasionally, parishioners express skepticism or negative views about the time and money their pastor invests in continuing education. In such situations, the pastor has the responsibility to demonstrate the value of continuing education by communicating to the congregation the connection between that education and improved performance in some aspect of ministry in that congregation. If that is not possible, the pastor may need to review the continuing education events that he gravitates toward and consider other directions for future study that would more directly benefit the present ministry.

The broad range of continuing education events available can be divided into two groups: those that teach techniques usable in ministry —vo-tech training—and those that challenge pastors to become whole persons so they can function effectively as parsons. A parson is the parish personage, the one whose wisdom represents the best values of the people of a community. Technique training includes such things as how to manage difficult people and how to conduct a stewardship campaign. Parson education ranges through Bible studies that connect the scriptures with contemporary life and seminars that work on self-understanding. Both kinds of continuing education are necessary, but periodic parson training, education for wholeness, is vital so that one's ministry continues to flourish. Ministry arising substantially out of techniques has limited effectiveness, especially if the pastor relying on them is not growing as a human being.

Clinical Pastoral Education (CPE) is now required by several denominations and encouraged by most others for their seminarians seeking ordination. CPE is taken in a hospital setting or occasionally a nursing home. The great value of CPE is that it integrates parson and technique education in a place where the people and their problems are real. Pastors who missed the opportunity for CPE during their seminary years may benefit from part-time programs offered by many hospitals.

The Leavening of Life

Pastors often become experts in certain aspects of their religious traditions, which is good. However, too much focus in the realm of religion, without the leavening of life in what parishioners call the real world, may lead parishioners to view their pastor as an incomplete personality, even if they would not express their feelings in these words. A pastor who devotes exclusive attention to a narrow range of theological subjects is practicing intellectual incest. Therefore, a pastor who explores and stays current in some subject of interest that is not church related will find additional, energizing opportunities through which to relate to parishioners. Parishioners will benefit, too, by seeing a more fully human person as their pastor.

At a minimum, a well-rounded pastor will pursue and stay current in at least two areas of special interest, one ecclesiastical and one secular. The more areas the pastor is capable of exploring in depth, the better, although the time commitments endemic to ministry make difficult the leisurely exploration of all subjects of interest to the pastor.

A Note about Spiritual Direction and Therapy

Formal education alone is not sufficient for the training and formation of a pastor. The world of ministry is full of brilliant scholars who are at best marginally competent at leading their congregations. On the other hand, some of the most effective, creative, and learned leaders I have known from various professions have been essentially self-taught, in some cases lacking even high school diplomas. Life experience is invaluable in the making of a pastor. The ability to connect paradigms, concepts, and theologies to the actually experienced lives of real people is not particularly valued in academia. Yet this skill is crucial for any pastor who would be successful.

For optimum pastoral growth, productive reflection is needed on life experiences, whatever they may be. Spiritual direction and psychotherapy are efficient and reliable ways of mediating life experience into life education.[1] As you are guided to reflect honestly on your behavior, relationships, desires, and beliefs, in addition to self-understanding, you learn a great deal that has direct application to parish ministry. Pastors who have learned something about their own motivations and fantasies better understand and more patiently accept the foibles and dreams of parishioners.

Meeting regularly with a spiritual director you trust and who challenges you is a worthwhile activity for any pastor. It is important as an educational experience for all pastors. Whether you are in crisis or not, whether emotionally healthy or not, psychotherapy, too, is useful for the educational value alone, apart from the healing dimension. For that reason I recommend psychotherapy for all pastors.

Of course, not all religious traditions are comfortable with the practice of spiritual direction. Some are hostile to it, claiming that it interferes with the direct relationship between the individual and God. Similarly, some people are suspicious of psychotherapy, believing it to be a faithless enterprise. Without rejecting either spiritual direction or psychotherapy, these critical views can help pastors evaluate the effectiveness of both activities. My experience is that both, in different ways, hold pastors accountable for the health of their ministries.

Spiritual direction and psychotherapy also act as correctives for each other. Spiritual direction is a religious enterprise, focusing on matters of faith. Some people who devote their lives to religious work develop subtle (and sometimes blatant) dualisms, in which they mentally divide the world into sacred and profane spheres. They tend to favor the sacred as the more worthy realm and want to exile themselves there. Unfortunately, some of these sacred spheres are constructed of fantasy and wishful thinking. And although a goal of spiritual direction is to connect religious insight with the whole of life as it is lived, a delusional religious foundation encourages this unhealthy dualistic thinking. The focus of psychotherapy is not restricted to what is considered sacred and can thus act as a corrective to keep pastors connected with a truly unified view of life. Conversely, psychotherapy can turn into a sterile, ultrarational exercise serving to alienate pastors from the treasures of their faith. Spiritual direction can correct this.

A Warning about Therapists

Since recommendations that pastors seek therapy occur throughout this book, a warning about therapists is warranted. Pastors must exercise care in selecting therapists, family counselors, and psychiatrists as well as spiritual directors. All the helping professions have significant numbers of dysfunctional practitioners. The dynamics that cause wounded people to be drawn to ministry apply to psychologists and social workers. In searching for healing for themselves, they seek to heal others.

People who have suffered psychological trauma or physical abuse can be good therapists. Indeed, they can be very skilled and effective. But the potential for deepened dysfunction is ever present when the wrong pastor and wrong therapist get together and the partnership feels so good. Pastor and therapist may feed off each other emotionally, luring the pastor away from reality and diminishing the chances for therapeutic improvement.

If the work with a therapist is not challenging, if it seems too easy or too painless, if it wanders aimlessly without results, or if it leads you down the therapist's personal pathway, you need to evaluate the relationship seriously. Discuss these concerns with the therapist, and if they are not satisfactorily resolved, seek another therapist. Of course, if a therapist makes any kind of sexual overture, don't bother evaluating the relationship. Get out fast.

Sex is usually an issue in therapy, beginning with the choice of a therapist. Some people are uncomfortable seeing a therapist of the opposite sex. For differing reasons, women and men alike experience misgivings about entrusting their vulnerabilities to opposite-sex therapists. If you have any hesitation about this matter, even if it's only a twinge of apprehension, by all means try to find a therapist of your own sex. If it really doesn't matter to you whether the therapist is male or female, well and good. But if it does, then don't jeopardize your therapeutic endeavor by building in, however slender, a layer of mistrust or anxiety.

Lifelong Learning

Pastors who make efforts to keep learning and stay current in matters sacred and profane do far better than those who rely on what they learned in seminary. Pastors who read widely—theology, novels, news magazines, food labels, clergy journals, catalogs, newspapers, parts of the Bible that do not appear in the lectionary, and so on—do better than pastors who read only commentaries and the scripture passages for next week's sermon.

How extensive is your reading? If it is limited, when are you going to visit the nearest public library? How old are your commentaries? Are you using only the reference books you acquired in seminary? When are you going to explore the wonderful resources published since then? How many magazines unrelated to ministry do you read regularly?

Poor education has many facets, all of which can jeopardize an otherwise good ministry. Lifelong learning is not a leisure time activity for pastors; it is an essential part of the calling.

CHAPTER 2

Culture Shock

In the world of parish ministry, pastors who succeed are well-thought-of, well-accepted and, over time, well-loved by their parishioners. They are also well-connected with their parishioners. One factor that can make this kind of wellness more difficult to achieve, however, is the culture shock that new pastors often experience as they encounter the social environment of their congregations.

Frequently, pastors and parishioners are born and raised in different worlds. Among mainline Protestants, for example, the majority of pastors have grown up in urban and suburban settings, typically as members of large congregations. They formed their expectations about ministry from their experiences in churches with many different programs and activities and a relatively high comfort level for diversity arising from the ethos of their metropolitan settings. Most congregations, on the other hand, are in small towns or rural areas and are relatively small in membership. Although the large churches do a good job of attracting women and men to the ministry, being few in number, they are not able to employ most of them. Since the small town and rural churches do not produce as many pastors, they must rely on pastors from the city.

This culture shock goes both ways. A rural congregation may be shocked and disoriented by its urbane, activist new pastor just as the pastor may be shocked and disappointed by the relaxed and insular ways of the parishioners. Of course, the congregation is more apt than the pastor to have had experience with this situation, having seen a series of pastors move in and out every few years. Many small town and rural congregations see part of their mission to be the training of inexperienced pastors (read that as urban-oriented pastors) in the true ways of parish ministry. Although this experience is quite common for recently ordained pastors, it can also happen to pastors with many years of service when they move from one cultural setting to another.

As a general rule, country congregations tend to be inward looking and oriented around family matters. The sense of community in such settings is highly personal, and the wants and needs of family members, whether members of the congregation or not, come before the program of the church. Metropolitan area congregations are more likely to be outward looking and more comfortable with diverse viewpoints, although there are many notable exceptions. They understand family not in terms of kinship but in the sense of interpersonal relationships beyond bloodlines and marriage. Members of a city congregation may perceive themselves as a family made up of individuals, while a country congregation may see itself as a church family made up of kinship families. Program (doing things, organizing activities) may be important in the urban church ethos, while family (belonging) is important in the country church ethos.

Congregations made up entirely (or nearly so) of people with a common racial identity may be very large, very small, or any size in between, regardless of the race. However, single-race congregations identified with a specific subgroup (particular language or nationality, social class, shade of skin color) tend to remain small. These subgroup congregations often present significant cultural adjustment challenges to pastors.

Shocking Moves

Culture shock can occur when moving to different regions of the country, too, even if the move is from rural church to rural church or urban church to urban church. A move from west to east or north to south for example, can be traumatic for both pastor and congregation. My experience is one of moving from Arizona, where the ethos is characterized by pioneer hospitality, openness to newcomers, frontier spirit, and high tolerance of individuality, to Pennsylvania, where the ethos includes the security of long-settledness, the primacy of families who have lived in the same place for generations, slow and careful acceptance of newcomers, and maintenance of traditions that have been well-proven over time. Four years passed before I felt comfortable in western Pennsylvania culture, and then I moved to central Pennsylvania and had to adjust to yet another ethos.

Colleagues who have moved around the United States from the Midwest to the Northeast and from the Northeast to the Southeast and from the South to the Far West have reported similar experiences of culture shock. Perhaps the universality of television lulls us into believing that we share one common culture with only variations in accent, but from Nome to Key West and from Labrador to southern California, we represent a thousand different cultures, some of which use languages other than English, notably Spanish, French, and many Native American tongues.

Geographic differences—topography, climate, vegetation—can intensify the effect of culture shock. When I moved to Pennsylvania, I was overwhelmed by countrysides of lush springtime greenness. I grew up with the comforting tans of the Arizona desert, the muted greens of palm trees, and the sweet scent of white orange blossoms in December. For years I experienced the bright greens of Pennsylvania as psychologically oppressive. Spring depressed me. Rather than hiking through politely spaced desert flora, I was surrounded by encroaching jungles of garish grasses and plants that were everywhere inescapable.

Over time I adjusted to the prodigal fertility of the land here, but it wasn't easy. Even now, after nearly two decades in the Northeast, my senses dilate with pleasant recognition of normality whenever I visit the Southwest. I am still connected emotionally to the land of my birth, and my experiences of the land have affected my attitudes and outlook on the world. There is a parable here for pastors whose ministry makes them sojourners in strange places.

The crucial thing for pastors to understand is that the culture and geography of a region have more influence on the beliefs and behaviors of parishioners than the denomination of the congregation. Presbyterians in North Dakota, for example, and Presbyterians in North Carolina may be part of the same denomination, but the ways they practice Presbyterianism in their respective places are different. A North Dakota Presbyterian may be more comfortable in a North Dakota Lutheran church than in a North Carolina Presbyterian church.

This is less true with churches characterized by withdrawal from or opposition to the larger society. Also, congregations with particular racial, ethnic, or language identities different from the surrounding community may function in reaction to rather than as reflections of the common culture and thus are exceptional. The great majority of congregations, however, exist in a context of regional culture.

A Note about Naiveté

A different kind of culture shock comes from the naiveté of many young pastors who have had little experience of the wider world. Many pastors entered ministry following this pattern: active participation in the youth program of the local church and some kind of church-related experience in college, leading to a sense of call to the ministry and beginning seminary upon graduation from college. This pattern tends to shelter the pastor-to-be from the trials and ugly realities of the world beyond, and not only the secular world, but also the world within the church.

In this regard, pastors who have come to ministry after having pursued other careers have an advantage over those who have known only the comfort and protection of school and seminary. I remember a class in pastoral care, in my senior year in seminary, in which the professor was describing the various problems and behaviors that parishioners would bring to us or hide from us when we reached our first congregations. The description was blunt, and the reaction to the professor's words came in two forms.

As it happened, the class was about evenly divided between students who had come to seminary right out of college and students who were seeking ministry as a second career. The second-career students responded by asking questions about how to deal with these situations, while the younger students denied that these problems would occur in the church. Oh, no, they protested, Christians don't do such things. People who come to church are all kindhearted, and their sins are all small ones. The things the professor described are done by people outside the church —or at least outside our denomination—they decided.

For a few pastors, such naiveté holds up to decades of challenge from parishioners who present themselves to their pastors in the worst possible circumstances, opening up their shadowed souls, baring their warts and scars, and confessing their dysfunctional behaviors, only to have their pastors dismiss or deny the depth of their sin and suffering. Most pastors, however, suffer all too deeply from the painful disillusionment of moving from the idealized world of the seminary to the real world of the parish.

All Ministry Is Local

Culture shock is not the fault of the pastor, who has no control over the existing ethos of the parish. But to do effective ministry, the pastor must enter the world of the parishioners who are being served. Depending on the denomination, the pastor has varying degrees of control over whether or not to accept the particular call. In any case, the pastor has the responsibility to learn as much as possible about the culture and ethos of the congregation to function optimally. Knowledge, awareness and, most of all, patience can help immeasurably in overcoming the trauma of culture shock.

Rephrasing Tip O'Neill's well-worn dictum, not only all politics, but all ministry is local. Global mission is local mission happening in places far from here. The focus of any ministry needs to be centered in a particular location. Pastors with global visions need to anchor their visions, focus them onto specific stages, and connect them imaginatively to the local scene. The world is a global village today, but the key word is *village*. Whether in Middletown, Pennsylvania, or Phayao, Thailand, ministry happens at the village level.

Pastors with worldviews different from their parishioners may respond in several ways. One common approach is to take a prophetic stand against the culture of the community. This generally leads them to short-term pastorates. Another tempting path is to become fully acculturated and affect the speech and attitudes of the local folk. This often results in a more comfortable pastorate, but it may rob the pastor of spiritual authority. Neither of these divergent ways equates with faithful ministry.

To be an effective leader, you don't have to take as your own the norms of the congregation you serve, but you do need to behave publicly in ways that don't ridicule the values of your congregation. You don't have to imitate the style or customs of your parishioners. In some cases, imitation may not be the sincerest form of flattery; instead, the people may perceive it as mockery. You must accept without judgment the reality of life as it is lived in the place where your ministry is grounded and meet the people where they are.

Here is a parable to consider. The first pastor preached to the congregation from a pew, saying only comfortable things that an average parishioner would say. The next pastor preached to the congregation from a soapbox down the street, saying disturbing things the congregation had trouble comprehending. You have come from a distant country to be the third pastor for this congregation. What will you do?

CHAPTER 3

Isolation

The expression "leave well enough alone" can apply in ironic ways to ministry. There is a sense in which a pastor needs to leave the congregation well enough alone, and the congregation needs to do the same for the pastor. Spiritual intimacy, which can develop between pastor and parishioners, and sensitive information, which comes to the pastor through pastoral counseling, require the pastor to maintain a certain emotional and professional distance from the people in the congregation. Another way of saying this is that the pastor needs to be well insulated from both the subtle and the brazen seductions of parishioners. At times of great vulnerability, members of congregations reveal their deepest needs and darkest secrets to their pastors. In the interest of developing closer bonds of affection, some parishioners want their pastors to reciprocate. Some pastors, with similar motivations, reveal their innermost selves to selected parishioners. This openness is a mistake.

Pastors get into trouble when they try to develop particular personal friendships with members of their congregations. Pastors should socialize with people they serve, but the process of developing a friendship demands an equality of relationship that can be problematic between pastor and parishioner.

The subject here is intimate (not sexual) relationships. Developing personal friendships is so self-revealing and time-consuming that a pastor who seeks to build a few such relationships among church members risks the perception among other parishioners of playing favorites. This perception, of course, can be disastrous when people take the next logical step and think that the pastor cares for a few favored people more than themselves, and therefore, either the pastor's judgment is flawed or those who are not favored are deficient in some way. And if a pastor is seen to play favorites with attractive members of the opposite sex, parishioners will imagine and gossip about all sorts of scandalous scenarios.

There is a trap, too, that can catch pastors who invest too much of their personal lives with selected parishioners. They become obliged to these parishioners in ways that diminish pastoral authority. Providing moral leadership to people who know in painful detail the flaws of the pastor becomes difficult. So, relationships of pastors with parishioners need to be cordial, warm, caring, even loving, but not selectively intimate.

Pastors need to show themselves as real human beings. Like everyone else, pastors are vulnerable, fallible people, and pretending otherwise is unhealthy. But how pastors reveal themselves—their insecurities, struggles, woundedness—is critical. Other chapters more fully develop this subject, but for now consider this: if self-disclosure is done openly (e.g., in preaching, teaching, or committee meeting settings), then much good can come of it. If done secretly with selected parishioners, danger abounds.

Inherent in the office of pastor are spiritual authority and power. Authority and power are abused when a pastor singles out a parishioner to reveal intimate matters, spiritual or otherwise, for the parishioner often hears this concomitant message: "You're special. You're different from the other members of this congregation. I trust you more than the others. I want you to have inside information." All too often this selective self-disclosure by a pastor is the opening round of a process of seduction, usually intentional.

Certainly, pastors need intimate and equal friendships, but they should find them outside the parish. Pastors moving to a new parish should resist targeting members for budding friendships and search for appropriate intimacies elsewhere. Inevitably, the life of a faithful pastor within the self-contained world of the congregation must entail some degree of isolation.

Hard Knocks and Unintended Messages

Other factors may heighten the sense of isolation in parish ministry. For example, in some congregations this matter of a pastor developing personal friendships with parishioners is not an issue because pastor and parishioners have little or nothing in common apart from the denomination to which they belong. In denominations that require extensive education for clergy, this distance can be extreme, as when a pastor with several graduate degrees serves a parish of blue-collar people. Typically, the values and interests of a seminary graduate are significantly different from those of one who has graduated from the school of hard knocks. Resentments can develop when the "hard knocks" person dismisses the "overeducated" pastor as a fancy thinker who doesn't know how to survive in the real world.

The reverse occurs when the seminary-educated pastor looks on the high school graduate as a crude thinker who fails to appreciate the important distinctions in theological or ethical matters that are obvious to anyone who would take the time to consider the pastor's position. Not that the pastor would actually say that to the parishioner, but such attitudes can be communicated subtly, through facial expressions, body language, or spoken signals. Raising eyebrows, for example, can communicate amusement or disbelief, especially if the pastor raises eyebrows while turning away from the parishioner. Crossing your arms while listening to someone conveys skepticism or a closed attitude. Certain phrases, such as "yes, yes" spoken rapidly, can seem dismissive. A pastor's tone of voice may reveal impatience or condescension. Most people are aware of these and many other examples of revelatory body language and speech patterns, but pastors need to exercise vigilance about these behaviors because they may contribute toward further isolation from their parishioners. When a pastor unwittingly sends negative signals through gestures or mannerisms, a barrier is built between pastor and people.

Since much nonverbal communication originates at the subconscious level, pastors are often unaware of sending unfriendly messages to their parishioners. One method for gaining awareness of how well they are communicating (apart from the content of their words) is for two pastors to monitor each other for a time. Each observes and provides feedback to the other about gestures, body language, speech patterns, and so on. For best results, the observing colleague should look for behaviors that communicate affirmative as well as negative messages. A good deal of nonverbal communication is positive in nature, enhancing pastoral effectiveness, and pastors need to know what serves them well as much as what serves them ill. Periodic remonitoring is a good idea, too, because personal behaviors are usually habitual, and habits (at least the bad ones) are hard to break.

Leaving Home

Pastors move to the parishes they serve, which means that most of the time they must leave their own homes to fulfill their callings. For a pastor who is called to a church that is far distant from the pastor's family and friends, that presents a different cultural ethos, and further, is a congregation where pastor and people have little in common, the sense of isolation can be overwhelming.

In places where the people are long settled, pastors are seen as significant transients whom the members need to accept, but often with reticence about nonchurch matters. After all, pastors come and go, while the people stay for generations. Thus, pastors play their roles as resident outsiders during their tenures, and their views on issues relating to the community are accordingly discounted. This adds yet another burden of loneliness to the lot of the pastor.

Let's make the situation even worse. Let's send a pastor to a church in a tiny town where the nearest colleague in the same denomination is fifty miles away, and the nearest neighboring pastor of any denomination is two miles away but belongs to a tradition which holds our pastor's denomination in contempt (or at least in grave suspicion). Not only that, but the nearest supermarket is an hour's drive from the church and the closest hospital (which is adequate but no more) is an hour away. The only library in the region is two hours away and disappointingly deficient in its collection. This situation may seem unusually bleak, but it is not rare, and I am aware of many that are much worse.

For an unmarried pastor, this scenario can be emotionally crushing, even for an introvert who savors solitude. A married pastor may do better, but risks in this isolated setting can harm the peace and tranquillity of the marriage. When pastor and spouse are forced to turn exclusively to each other for all their social needs, all their perceptions of life in the parish, all their mutual nurturing and intimate conversation, problems can develop for both people. Resentments may arise as unmet needs simmer. Little slights may take on large significance. When the pastor goes off to distant meetings of denominational committees or off to another state for continuing education, the spouse left alone at home or at work in the community may feel unhappy or jealous.

Clergy spouses who are employed outside the home, male or female, seem to handle isolation better than those who work at home. And those in metropolitan areas seem to have fewer problems in this regard than those in rural areas. Nevertheless, homemaker spouses (the great majority of whom are female) are often forced by circumstance to provide pastoral care for their pastor-spouses without having their own friends or pastors to turn to.

My pastor-to-pastors job description specifically includes spouses and children of pastors. Repeatedly, I have heard wives of pastors say that in all the years their husbands have been pastors, my position marks the first time since they married that they have had a pastor of their own. I have not heard this sentiment from male spouses of pastors, so there may be some differences in experience between male and female clergy spouses. As clergy husbands become more numerous, research needs to be done on their experiences compared with the large body of material on clergy wives.

The Differentness of Pastors

Pastors may experience relative degrees of isolation, ranging from the necessary emotional distance required for consistent and effective ministry to extreme geographical and cultural exile from family, friends, and colleagues. A pastor who does not experience some sense of isolation in a parish setting may lack the empathy needed for this calling. One spark that fuels good ministry is this aching feeling of distance that creates a need for intimacy with God.

People who are ordained to pastoral ministry are by definition set apart to pursue this need for intimacy with God on behalf of the people of the congregation. Thus, pastors are seen as different from other people. My observation is that pastors reject this notion of differentness. While accepting responsibility for the ministry of the laity (in varying degrees according to ecclesiastical tradition), many folks in the pews recognize that their pastors are not like them. It is not that they are qualitatively superior to other people, or spiritually superior for that matter, but pastors tend to be different from the general population in various ways. Pastors frequently see and hear things that most people do not see and hear. They think about things, events, and relationships in ways that most people do not.

In my experience, women and men who understand themselves to be called by God to ordained ministry have personal qualities that differ from societal norms. Regardless of what age they entered ordained service, most pastors have from childhood experienced being set apart, being misunderstood, or thinking about ordinary things in unusual ways. No single personality type is common to all pastors, but a sense of isolation based on being different from "normal people" is common among them.

One cost of pastoral ministry is the isolation inherent in this differentness. Pastors must accept it about themselves and affirm it as a gift from God. Rather than feel shame or remorse about it, pastors would do well to celebrate their distinctiveness as it has been confirmed in their ordinations. In a sense, the setting apart of a person for ministry that occurs symbolically in ordination is an act of recognition of the isolating peculiarities that God conferred on the ordinand at birth or in childhood. These differences bear fruit in the faithful practice of parish ministry.

All of this means that pastors need to find healthy ways of dealing with the reality of isolation. As noted above, developing friendships outside the parish is important. For a variety of reasons, such as geographical distances, this may be difficult to accomplish, but nurturing such relationships needs to become a high priority for pastors and spouses.

Invest time in correspondence or money in periodic long-distance telephone calls. Build into your calendar regular appointments with a colleague or nonparish friend. You can realize many blessings through refreshment and connectedness with the world beyond the walls of parish ministry. If you can be flexible with vacation and study leave time, develop a creative schedule to maximize connectedness with family and friends away from the parish. Taking a week of vacation every three months, for example, may help you break your fast of isolation often enough to make the rest of the months tolerable.

The Lone Eagle

The most pernicious form of isolation, and the one that is most likely to get pastors in trouble, is self-imposed. I call it the lone eagle mentality. Some pastors operate in isolation, making decisions by themselves, doing everything (or as much as they can get away with) by themselves. These pastors do not encourage parishioners to participate in the work of the church. The pastors will see to all the details. In extreme cases, lone eagle pastors will not delegate work to associates or other employees in the parish.

This behavior ranges from seemingly innocuous things such as the pastor's taking responsibility for turning on the lights in the church on Sunday morning to excessively controlling behavior in which the pastor oversees and authorizes every aspect of congregational life. Control, of course, is usually the goal of this isolationist behavior. One example is the senior pastor of a multiple staff church who controls access to the congregation's personnel committee. "No member of the staff is allowed to talk to the personnel committee without consulting with me first," this pastor proclaims. A subtler but no less controlling variation is for the head-of-staff pastor to sit in on all personnel committee meetings when other staff members are interviewed. The free exchange of feelings and concerns is thus hampered.

Controlling access to mail can also be a lone eagle tactic. Some pastors insist on seeing first all the mail that comes into their parishes. They are then able to decide which communications reach staff, board members, church school teachers, and so on. These pastors may conveniently discard denominational and ecumenical correspondence dealing with matters they do not care about, thus isolating the congregation from the larger church. Several pastors I know have gone so far as to hide mail addressed to board members. In one case a cache of mail was discovered in the trunk of an abandoned car after the pastor left that parish.

Lone eagle pastors who consistently make their decisions in isolation tend to make poor decisions. The more isolated the decision-making process, the more opportunity for the pastors to become disconnected from reality. Especially with matters of sensitivity or controversy, pastors need to consult with colleagues and lay leaders, gather information, and check out their assumptions and ideas with others before acting.

My observation is that pastors who serve parishes in remote areas are at even greater risk in this regard because isolated communities tend to be out of touch with the wider world and thus suffer distorted world-views. An individual congregation off by itself out in the country may perceive the regional governing body or denomination in ways inconsistent with the common reality of the larger group. Such congregations may distrust all outside institutions, especially ecclesiastical ones. The danger is that pastors can be drawn into these systems of isolation and assume the distorted views of reality of their parishioners. Indeed, all pastors need to be wary of being co-opted by parishioners who have private agendas and warped views of other people and the larger society. The more isolated the congregation—by geography, culture, language, or theology—the more alert the pastors must be to this phenomenon.

Keeping in contact with colleagues and others beyond the parish system becomes a matter of staying in touch with reality. Mental health is also at stake. When pastoral isolation is prolonged and the inevitable additional stresses of ministry accumulate, paranoia sometimes develops. And decisions made out of paranoid states are certain to be flawed, thus creating even more problems.

Western religious traditions understand the call to ministry this way: God communicates with an individual person, revealing God's desire for that particular person to become a pastor, a teacher, a prophet, or something else. The ranks of clergy are filled with pastors who believe that they have been singled out and called by God by name to be ordained for ministry. A strong vision of what one's ministry should be like usually accompanies the sense of call. There is, of course, truth in this understanding, but there is also a dangerous side to it. Ego-inflating implications reinforce any lone eagle tendencies that may already be present.

Rather than foster an ethos that celebrates individualism and the idiosyncratic search for prophetic power, I believe denominations and seminaries would do better to emphasize calls to ministry as part of the larger economy of God. Cooperative clerical enterprises could be given greater recognition. It would not deny the personal nature of God's call to each person, but it could alleviate a little of the competitiveness that many pastors feel among colleagues. Likewise, greater recognition of the ministry of all the people of God would help pastors keep things in perspective. Although pastors are ordained to particular functions, these functions do not represent the totality of ministry. Some pastors seem to need strong reminders from their denominations of their responsibilities to equip the saints for ministry, and many are not getting it.

The Pastor as Hired Servant

An interesting twist on the lone eagle phenomenon occurs when people in a parish view the pastor as a hired servant whom they pay to take care of all the details of church life, including a long inventory of tasks parishioners could easily do themselves. One reason for this may be that previous pastors did everything and discouraged members from rightful participation in the wider ministry of the congregation. A small church, for example, may expect the pastor to act as church secretary and custodian. A large church may hire additional staff to take care of things that are not being done. The underlying assumption is that the congregation pays its staff to do the work of the church, and the responsibilities of the members (or leaders among members) consist only of making decisions about the work that the staff does. This situation constrains the ministry of the church and has adverse implications for a pastor's effective use of time, anchoring the pastor to the parish without cooperative support from the congregation. This, in turn, makes it difficult for a pastor to meet personal needs for intimacy and friendship outside the parish.

Institutional Incest

Overworked pastors in high-expectation churches are vulnerable to getting caught up in institutional incest. Pastors who have very little time to take care of personal needs outside the congregation turn to certain influential members or a particular church school class or a prayer group to meet emotional needs. As often as not, the pastors are seduced into intimate association by members of such groups. As a result, pastors become even more isolated from the larger community, from colleagues, and from healthy friendships outside the closed world of the particular congregation (or small part of the congregation).

This incest is not necessarily a sexual phenomenon, but it is not unusual for these relationships to become sexual. Accounts of young adult Sunday school classes or church fellowship groups becoming incubators for divorce and remarriage to others within the group are common. Stories of multiple affairs and spouse swapping by members of these groups are not rare. Pastors are not immune from involvement in these dynamics, and isolation is a factor that makes pastors more susceptible to them.

A Note about Time

Albert Einstein taught humankind that time is relative. Because of this, astronauts in space, we are told, age more slowly than people on earth. What is demonstrably clear is that the human experience of time is relative. A person in love, for example, perceives the passing of time differently while awaiting a visit from the beloved than when in the presence of the beloved.

Time is relative in parish ministry, too. All hours are not equal. An hour spent consoling a distraught parishioner is longer than an hour spent perusing a Bible commentary. It is longer in the sense of being more intense and more taxing. Ten hours of emotionally charged pastoral work in a week may be equivalent to fifty hours of routine work in terms of a pastor's expenditure of energy. Many pastors are diligent about monitoring the amount of time they devote to ministry, making sure they take a day off regularly. Some, however, fail to take into account the relative intensity of their time. The need for rest and recharging is more a factor of the nature of the hours in ministry than the number of the hours.

There are those in ministry who feel guilty if they do not work sixty hours a week. Some of these pastors have become angry, frustrated, defensive, or depressed because their congregations do not appreciate their long hours of labor. The problem here is that the quantity of the time is not nearly as important to parishioners as the quality of it.

Effective pastors are engaged in their work but not enmeshed in it. To survive with grace over the long term, pastors need to learn how to use time to best advantage. Days, weeks, or seasons of intensity should be tempered with periods of intentional respite. Discovering the right rhythm, which takes into account the dissonance of unexpected events, is a primary and lifelong task for all pastors.

When there simply is not enough time in the day or week or month to accomplish everything on the list, prioritize ruthlessly. Careful evaluation of that agenda will probably reveal a number of time-consuming things that do not really need to be done. Think about what would happen if certain things were delayed indefinitely or never done. If the honest conclusion is that nothing adverse would occur, let go of them.

At the other end of the continuum from pastors who work too much are those who are not fully engaged and who do not give enough time to their ministries. It is widely known but seldom acknowledged that pastors serving full-time positions in small parishes can coast for years, doing minimal work, if they are so inclined. Undisciplined pastors in large parishes likewise find it easy to hide from the demands of the day because most parishioners assume the pastor must be caring for someone else or tending to some major project.

However, pastors who consistently fail to cover the basics in parish ministry eventually find themselves saying good-bye to congregations that are glad to see them go. The farewell receptions that congregations hold for such pastors are strange and sad events, characterized by forced good humor and furtive glances of relief that the end is near.

Unproductive pastors need to find ways to become more engaged in the tasks of ministry. At the same time, excessively responsible pastors need to learn moderation. For the great majority who would locate themselves at points in between the extremes on this continuum, appropriate personal evaluation is in order.

Intimacy and Boundaries

Pastors would do well to recognize that they don't have to do it all alone. The ministry of the congregation belongs to the whole congregation. Pastors who would take on a disproportionate share of that ministry need to let go, and parishioners who would place a disproportionate share on their pastors need to be educated about their own responsibilities.

Underlying the various kinds of isolation that have been described in this chapter are two issues: the need for intimacy and the maintenance of boundaries. These are often experienced in tension with each other. Pastors have the same needs for intimate relationships as parishioners, but they must not seek to satisfy those needs with parishioners. Yet, often there is temptation or even encouragement from members of congregations for pastors to cross boundaries and be intimate with parishioners in unhealthy or inappropriate ways. In the final analysis, the responsibility for preserving professional distance falls to the pastors.

Some kind of isolation in parish ministry is inevitable. Ministry is a lonely calling. Still, you can find healthy and creative ways of dealing with the loneliness of the pastor's life. Acknowledgment of the isolation to yourself and to colleagues is a good first step. The next step is to make an inventory of isolating factors and isolating personal behaviors. Write down things noted in this chapter that apply, plus any others that come to mind. Then divide the list into three categories: things external to you that cannot be changed, things external to you that can be modified or improved, and things over which you have direct control.

Step three is to let go of everything in category one and go to work on categories two and three. Meditate, reflect, pray, talk with other people, look around, and consider the possibilities.

CHAPTER 4

Hobbyhorses and Unpaid Dues

To foster well-rounded personalities, pastors were encouraged in the chapter on poor education to develop interests beyond those related to ministry. However, whether related to ministry or not, some pastors carry their interests to such lengths that they become identified with their subjects almost exclusively. They seek to become well armed with regard to some compelling issue and end up being well worn, wearing out their welcomes. The subject here is hobbyhorses. Some issues, frequently associated with causes or social movements or religious doctrines, capture the imaginations of clergy (and many other people as well).

It does not matter what the hobbyhorse is. It does not matter how right (or how left) the issue is. There is a difference between being an expert in some area and being so fully caught up in a cause that objectivity is completely lost. Some pastors are so connected to their hobbyhorses that when they rise to speak in denominational meetings, their colleagues know in advance what they intend to speak about. On occasion when a subject is raised with which these pastors are associated, coleagues may even know in advance exactly what these hobbyists will say.

Still, in ecclesiastical organizations beyond the parish level, in settings dominated by clergy, there is a high tolerance for ministerial hobbyhorses. They are assigned to the realm of the prophetic, and colleagues admire many pastors for their quixotic witness or prophetic actions. Certainly, churches need people who are willing to take bold stands on difficult issues. Justice, equality, interpretation of scriptures, and so on are all compelling matters for which, necessarily and rightfully, champions arise.

Problems arise, however, when hobbyhorses collide with the demands of parish ministry. When the hobbyhorse becomes so important or so time consuming that the ordinary demands of the parish seem unimportant or less worthy, big trouble looms. Parishioners expect pastors to tend to their spiritual needs. Religious traditions have differing expectations of what that means in terms of specific pastoral activities, but a few basic pastoral functions have become normative in the current era in North America.

Paying Dues

Tending to these basic pastoral functions is known as paying your dues (or paying the rent or taking care of baby). With greater or lesser emphasis depending on the particular denominational traditions and the demographics of the particular congregation, these basic functions are being a thoughtful worship leader (which includes effective preaching to a greater or lesser extent depending on the denomination); tending to the rites of the Church (marriages, baptisms, funeral services, etc.); making timely hospital and crisis visits; praying with and for parishioners in services of worship, church meetings, and visitations; being approachable and regularly available to parishioners for counsel; calling on older people, especially the homebound members of the congregation; and conducting oneself in public in a manner that brings no embarrassment to the congregation.

Preaching carries widely varying importance to parishioners depending on how well other activities are performed. Some pastors can preach mediocre sermons week after week with few complaints from their parishioners. These pastors are otherwise paying their dues. Other pastors preach consistently outstanding sermons yet receive sharp criticism about poor preaching. My observation is that when members of a congregation perceive they are not being cared for by their pastor, they focus more attention on the pastor's public pronouncements, especially the sermons. If they feel slighted in other ways, they will look for things in the sermons to pick apart, commonly distorting or magnifying out of proportion what was actually said.

Office Hours for Miss Emily

In some church cultures, office hours are part of the pastoral dues. Frequently in small town and suburban churches, parishioners expect the pastor to be available in the office or study at appointed times during the week. If someone gets the notion to stop by to see the pastor, barring an emergency, the pastor will be there, ready to talk. Appointments are not necessary. Sometimes it is an unspoken expectation.

Miss Emily belongs to such a church. She stopped by her suburban church office a few weeks ago and saw her new pastor chatting with the church secretary. "Oh, good, you're here," she said. "I need to talk with you."

The pastor, who was taking a break from intensive work on next week's sermon, smiled at Miss Emily and said, "Certainly, dear. You can make an appointment with the secretary." Then the pastor turned and walked back to the study. No doubt the pastor was preoccupied with the sermon text and had forgotten about the matter within five minutes. But Miss Emily will remember the pastoral snub for years to come.

The importance of pastoral visitation varies according to the relative age of a congregation. The boomer generation—now in midlife—isn't much interested in pastoral home visits, but the World War II generation of their parents still places a high value on social calling—what many pastors dismiss as hand-holding—and these older parishioners do not hesitate to complain if they perceive dereliction in this significant pastoral duty.

As the boomer generation ages and the World War II generation passes to the church triumphant, shifts will inevitably occur in what congregations expect from their pastors. The specific dues will change, but dues will always be required.

My sense is that congregational expectations about pastoral care (not including social visitation) have increased over the last two decades. Parishioners now routinely go to their pastors for counseling and support in everything from marital problems to Alzheimer's disease. Grief work, hospice care, long-term disability concerns, nursing home admissions, financial problems, sexual matters, and more are brought to pastors by parishioners who expect their pastors to know how to help. Parishioners evaluate pastors on the basis of how well they provide an ever-broadening service called pastoral care.

Traditional pastoral care duties, such as hospital and bereavement visits, remain the standard for judging a pastor's performance. Parishioners take such visits seriously and will talk about them for years. They will also remember anticipated pastoral care visits that did not happen. They will remember that the pastor did not come over to the house the day Papa called the church office with the news he had cancer. That day will stay in their memories for decades.

A Note about Embarrassment

It is only natural that a congregation would want its pastor to be well-considered in the larger community. Members of the congregation work and socialize with people who are members of other churches as well as with unchurched people. The pastor represents the congregation, as a figurehead, to the whole neighborhood, town, or city. Therefore, the pastor must do nothing that would bring embarrassment to the people of the congregation. This is true no matter where the parish is located, but especially true for small towns and rural areas where nearly all the pastors are known by face and reputation.

Several items previously discussed in this and earlier chapters can be sources of embarrassment. These relate to hobbyhorses, paying dues, and cultural norms, and pastors frequently fail to recognize them as such. I have heard many complaints about pastors and pastors' spouses breaking the (usually unspoken) dress codes of their parishes by appearing in public in, for example, short shorts, jeans, tee shirts, or jogging suits. Members of the congregation may appear in public in such attire, but pastors are expected to dress more conservatively. The embarrassment comes when a member of another congregation comments to a member of the pastor's congregation about the pastor's "inappropriate" appearance at a local restaurant or the hospital or a service club meeting.

Whether the cultural norms of the community are reasonable or fair is another matter. The problem for pastors is that breaking them publicly brings embarrassment to members of the congregation.

Alcohol consumption by pastors is a particularly volatile subject in some communities. Some denominations have strong traditions against alcohol use, while others are more tolerant. Nevertheless, regardless of the denomination, pastors who are seen in bars or liquor stores may bring embarrassment to their parishioners. Because of this, many pastors travel to other towns to buy their dinner wine and other alcoholic beverages. The event that is most likely to present alcohol-related embarrassing possibilities is the wedding reception. If alcohol is served, the pastor must be very careful about drinking it. Drinking to the point of becoming tipsy is certain to be noticed and will be talked about beyond the parish because wedding guests almost always include people from outside the congregation.

Not paying dues can bring embarrassment in certain circumstances. The failure to visit Aunt Bea in the nursing home, for example, may reflect negatively on the congregation because the whole town knows and loves Aunt Bea. When Aunt Bea's pastor does not call on her, people from beyond the congregation will comment on this lapse. Even though the criticism is directed at the pastor and not the congregation, members of the congregation will still feel embarrassed because their pastor is publicly perceived as deficient in some way.

Hobbyhorses can sometimes cause embarrassment, too. If pastors become publicly associated with issues that are not generally supported in the community, or if they behave in ways perceived as radical or extreme, embarrassment will redound to their congregations. More often, however, the embarrassment comes because the hobbyhorse takes up so much pastoral time that people see the congregation as being ill-served.

Congregations do not like being embarrassed. Sometimes parishioners behave in ugly ways when they feel embarrassed by their pastor's behavior. Parishioners' expectations about a pastor's deportment may be unreasonable, unrealistic, and ungracious, or they may be right on target. Regardless of what parishioners' expectations may be, you need to be sensitive to factors that may cause embarrassment. This is not to say that your primary motivation in ministry should be the avoidance of controversy, but a little discretion and a lot of careful thought about the implications of public actions will serve you well.

Visiting Aunt Bea

Pastors who pay their dues are generally well thought of and well loved, and their congregations are well disposed to give them leeway in pursuing hobbyhorses. That is, pastors who tend to the basics of ministry consistently and faithfully, and who do so in a positive spirit, do not usually get into trouble for pursuing their concerns or causes. Pastors who pay their dues faithfully but with even a modicum of resentment, however, do not receive the same latitude in pursuing personal issues. No matter how often a pastor visits Aunt Bea in the nursing home, if this pastoral task is approached as a chore that has to be gotten out of the way in order to play, that message will eventually be communicated to the congregation. Affected mannerisms and impatient gestures, no matter how subtle, will register on the collective unconscious of the congregation if repeated often enough.

Well-mannered behavior is expected of pastors, even with disagreeable people, and being polite sometimes means finding a way to be interested in Aunt Bea's story about Cousin Dorothy the forty-seventh time she tells it. Paying your dues means hearing her out because she is a child of God and deserves pastoral care and affection. This is different from phony caring, which is acted out like a role in a play.

Through habit, some pastors fall into a stylized method of responding to pastoral care situations. They assume a certain tone of voice, which is followed by sounds of sympathy and a pattern of familiar pious words. They offer gestures—a pat on the shoulder, a squeeze of the hand —and say a prayer. None of this is bad, but if the automatic response becomes essentially the same for everything from simple aggravations to profound tragedy, parishioners will question the pastor's sincerity.

No pastor can be fully present with all parishioners at all times, but there is such a thing as spiritual authenticity. Even in agonizing moments when one really wants to be doing something else—something more important than listening to Aunt Bea the forty-eighth time—that authenticity or phoniness will manifest itself in some way. One cannot hide forever, and though the odds are favorable for getting away with it for a while, eventually, the congregation will uncover and gossip about phoniness.

It all comes down to this: If a pastor can tend to all the basics of ministry with authenticity most of the time, then opportunities for prophetic ministry will be tolerated, even valued, by members of the congregation. A classic example is the young pastor who publicly opposed the Viet Nam War during the late 1960s. The conservative midwestern congregation was confronted the pastor's antiwar sermons from time to time, but not every month. Many members were veterans of World War II who were not sympathetic to draft dodgers and peaceniks. And they did not like their pastor's participation in peace marches. But they did not protest the peace work, and despite the activism, they loved and supported their pastor.

This pastor faithfully paid parish dues first, and they all knew it. When the crusty American Legion member was in the hospital with heart disease, the pastor was by his side praying for him nearly every day. The parishioners were secure in the love their pastor showed them, and they recognized that they did not have to agree with him on every issue to love him back. The reverse is also true.

If a pastor finds it difficult or impossible to tend to the basics, then the pastor is not suited for parish ministry and needs to find some other calling. If the hobbyhorse—the pet project, social concern, theological issue, prophetic activity—becomes so overwhelming that it takes precedence over the day-to-day life of the congregation, then it has become a professional racehorse, and perhaps God is calling the pastor who is consumed by the matter to leave the parish and chase after it.

Pastors and Prophets

What begins as a hobby issue may develop into a genuine prophetic calling. If so, there is a price to be paid. The prophets known to us through scripture did not cling to secure positions. They did not proclaim their messages from protected offices within hierarchies. Rather, they stood outside their institutions and spoke their prophetic words with personal integrity. Prophetic preaching and urging parishioners to support matters of justice are appropriate pastoral functions. However, pastors who would be true prophets must be willing to give up the comfort and security of the pastoral office.

Parishioners deserve to be well tended and spiritually well fed by their pastors. Indeed, they need this care in order to carry on *their* ministry in and for the Church and the world where they live and work. Pastors who underfeed their parishioners in order to feed their own hobbyhorses will sooner or later get bitten by hungry and resentful parishioners.

CHAPTER 5

Theological Agendas

Without question pastors need to be well versed in the scriptures and other literature of their traditions. And it is certainly a plus for ministry when pastors have a well-developed and consistent theological framework out of which to respond to the needs and crises of life. However, sometimes this "well-versedness" gets in the way of effective ministry, and sometimes it is misused in harmful ways.

Theology and ministry are not the same thing, although they are overlapping enterprises. Theology is the art of discerning the nature of God and exploring the implications of that discernment for humankind. Ministry is the art of mediating the passion and will of God among people. Both theology and ministry need rules and discipline in order to be developed effectively. Ultimately, however, as with the writing of good poetry, sometimes the rules (but not the discipline) need to be set aside for the sake of the art.

Some poems are technically correct, perfectly conforming to all the rules of the genre, and yet they fail as art because they are trite or lack spirit. For poetry, choosing exactly the right word is more important than conforming to formal requirements. The poet must exercise passionate discipline in making choices of content over form. So, too, with ministry. Content is the expression of present experience, while form represents age-old institutional traditions. Pastors may follow carefully all the doctrines and rules of their traditions—be excellent theologians— and yet not succeed in parish ministry. Following the rules is easier than exercising disciplined thought and action in the present arena of human life, and so pastors are sometimes tempted to fall back on the rules rather than do the hard work of pastoral ministry—searching for the right word—in the ambiguous arena of real life.

The goal of discipline in ministry is to be able at any given moment to express passionately or compassionately the presence and will of God in the immediacy of unfolding life. The goal of following the rules is to contain that expression in a safe, tautological world. The rules are usually wise and worthy of respect but not universally applicable. Therefore, as disciples within their traditions, pastors need to give the greater weight to discipline in order to be more effective.

Relating to Parishioners

Sound pastoral care does not depend on whether the pastor's theological views are conservative, centrist, or liberal. What does matter is how the pastor relates to people in situations involving the application of theology or doctrine. The practice of parish ministry, therefore, is not as much about right belief as about right relationship.

When a pastor relates to people out of a theological agenda rather than out of common humanity, misunderstanding and resentment are bound to occur. When a pastor consistently evaluates people based on their faithfulness to the doctrine of their Church or the degree of their acceptance of the pastor's particular theological views, the health of the parish is in jeopardy.

A pastor who believes that the most significant job is dispensing right doctrine is in danger of sabotaging chances of educating parishioners in sound theology. If the message is more important to the pastor than the people who are to benefit from the message, the pastor needs to turn around that perspective.

The Idolatry of Doctrine

Theology has been called the queen of the sciences, and in many traditions God is described metaphorically as a monarch. These are positions of superiority, and pastors may fall into the trap of assuming positions of superiority based on their knowledge of and enthusiasm for the theologies and doctrines of the religious institutions they serve. Pastors must value the enterprise of theological debate and discernment or else they could not be pastors, but if they place their own doctrinal or theological stances (or their institution's) above the common reality of the people, they are making a mistake.

Let me be clear about this. The error is idolatry. Too often pastors succumb to the temptation to make idols of their theology or doctrine. They worship their own particular understanding of the nature of God rather than worship God. Sometimes this happens because of the psychological needs of the pastor, for example, the need to control other people or the need to gain some control over the chaos within the pastor's mind.

The field of religion is a breeding ground for idolatry, and the traditions that crusade the hardest against idolatries seem to produce a disproportionate share of them. Making an idol of the Bible is an especially pernicious example, but I have seen liturgy, creeds, process, and even therapy function as idols of worship. Religious ideologues of any stripe make poor pastors and can be particularly destructive of the peace and unity of congregations. Such people are better suited to prophetic ministries. In parish settings, ideologues operate by attracting core groups of like-minded followers who then form a defensive shield around their leader. Ideologue pastors are frequently adept at divide-and-conquer techniques to gain functional control of congregations.

A theology built on a confident faith tends to be flexible. The more anxiety in the mind of the believer, the more rigid the theology tends to be. Pastors get into trouble when their theology is narrow or shallow and rigidly held. They demonstrate their limitations and are incapable of relating creatively, constructively, or compassionately to their parishioners. They can also have problems if their theology is deep and complex but bound within too narrow a context. An example would be claiming that God is in relationship with only the people who believe what "we" believe.

Theological Malpractice

Here are some specific examples of theological malpractice. Some pastors like to settle differences or set parishioners straight by quoting scripture at them. This practice is commonly known as hitting them over the head with the Bible. Certainly, clergy are not the only people guilty of it, but some pastors have honed it to a fine art.

In addition to using the Bible as a weapon, some pastors verbally clobber their parishioners with defiant citations from denominational constitutions and other ecclesiastical literature. There is an adversarial quality to the way they use the resources of their religious traditions in order to prove others wrong or control their actions. Too often hurt feelings and resentments result. Besides that, the more adversarial the use of scripture, the more likely the pastor is creating arguments out of context or distorting the message of the passage for personal reasons.

Another troubling practice is using scripture or prayer as a tool for intervention in disagreements. Again, control is usually the motive. Here's how it happens: A church board or committee is struggling with some matter of controversy. The discussion becomes heated. Suggestions arise that challenge the agenda or position of the pastor, so the pastor intervenes by citing verses of scripture dealing with peace or harmony. The object is to induce guilt in the contrary parties and thus bring them into cooperation with the pastor's agenda. Frequently, it works—in the short run. But over time, if this behavior is repeated, others experience it as manipulation.

A pastor may intervene with prayer at the crucial moment when the discussion is most heated just before a resolution or decision can be made. The prayer then subtly focuses guilt on those who have had the temerity to challenge, question, or otherwise oppose the agenda of the pastor—all in the name of peace and unity and how God would want them (phrased as "us") to behave.

A more frequent misuse of prayer occurs when a pastor says, "Let us pray," and proceeds to preach rather than beseech. Such "prayers" can be identified by the declarative nature of the words coming from the pastor's mouth. Ostensibly addressed to God, these words are actually affirmations, instructions, or advice to the assembled folk. Preaching prayers are commonly offered on many occasions, not only in conflict situations. I believe that pastors who preach in prayers do not intend insult to their congregations and are not aware that they are doing it. Most pray this way out of habit based on an unfortunate choice of a role model for how a pastor should pray in public.

Certainly, scripture and prayer can be appropriately used during controversies and disagreements, but timing and selection are critical. In the midst of disagreements, for example, rather than cite verses that stress peace, why not take comfort in verses about the struggles that the people of God have experienced, the controversies and disagreements they have encountered and have lived.to tell about? Consider some of the experiences described in Exodus, Judges, and Job, as well as Acts and Revelation. Rather than prematurely intervene with prayer before the climax of a disagreement, thus preempting the natural resolution, let the process unfold to its conclusion, be it resolution or impasse, and then pray.

Another area where theological agendas can be used in harmful ways is pastoral counseling. From celebrating the birth of a child to grief counseling after the death of a loved one, pastors are called to care for their parishioners through joy and pain and everything in between. They often counsel with parishioners about their doubts, fears, sins, losses, major decisions, and most intimate feelings. Parishioners rely on their pastors to be knowledgeable about the stance of their faith tradition on the matters they are struggling with and also to be compassionate and gentle with them in the midst of their angst. Thus, pastors who have worked through and come to clear understandings about what they believe and what their traditions hold about the basic issues of life—the problem of evil, the nature of God, the nature of humankind—are better poised to provide comfort and assurance to confused or troubled parishioners. And the more secure they are in their beliefs, the more accepting they can be in responding to the insecurities of their parishioners.

Theological Struggling and Personal Disclosure

This is not to say that pastors should avoid personal spiritual struggling or wrestling with their doubts. Their spiritual growth and health depend on their continuing to struggle, think, reflect, pray, and rethink, re-reflect, and repray about theological and doctrinal matters. But they should be sensitive about inflicting their personal struggles on their parishioners, who may be searching on a different plane or at another level of sophistication. Pastors experiencing personal crises may want to theologize about their situations in their sermons. Unless done with careful discipline, such preaching can turn into verbal emotional bleeding, which confuses parishioners, seriously troubling some.

In *Being Clergy, Staying Human,* Dorothy McRae-McMahon writes, "There is a fine line between the trusting sharing of the human struggle and an inappropriate and unhealthy need for self-disclosure of one's private life."[1] McRae-McMahon provides extensive guidance on the appropriate ways pastors can remain open and honest with their congregations. Other pastor-authors have written of their theological struggles and personal lives, which can be useful models for the rest of us. Daniel T. Hans has written movingly in *God In the Witness Stand: Questions Christians Ask In Personal Tragedy* about his three-year-old daughter's death from cancer while he was pastor of a congregation in Connecticut.[2] Frederick Buechner's autobiographical trilogy, *The Sacred Journey*, *Now and Then*, and *Telling Secrets*, is another good source of insight.[3] In *Telling Secrets* Buechner writes, "It is important to tell at least from time to time the secret of who we truly and fully are—even if we tell it only to ourselves—because otherwise we run the risk of losing track of who we truly and fully are."[4]

There is another side to the story, however. Pastors who deal with their personal struggles in sermons can be misheard or misinterpreted by parishioners, leading to harmful rumors and gossip. Upon hearing the pastor acknowledge sinfulness, some people will immediately suspect sexual involvements. I once alluded in a sermon to my youthful misdeeds while in the army, without naming the specific sins. One parishioner was convinced he knew exactly what I had done, although what he thought was not correct. He interpreted my sins according to his own, and I was not able to convince him (in private conversation) that I had not done what he had done. Some of this misinterpretation is inevitable and not harmful, but the remedy for the worst of it is careful preparation of your words leading to clear explanation of any personal matters dealt with in sermons or other public presentations.

What really hurts parishioners, though, is a pastor's use of the congregation as a forum for rationalization or personal therapy. A pastor going through a divorce, for example, may be tempted to use the sermon repeatedly to emote about the pain or injustice of it all. A pastor in the midst of a midlife crisis may try to rationalize personal improprieties by theologizing about them in sermons.

This tendency can be even more pronounced in pastoral counseling settings. Pastors in the midst of spiritual crises or theological struggles may tell their problems to individual parishioners, in essence outdoing whatever problems the parishioners bring to them. This, of course, is a disservice to the counselees, but there is yet a worse practice. Some pastors reveal their improprieties to selected parishioners in a "you tell me your sins and I'll tell you mine" fashion. They do this as a way to rationalize away their own actions while supposedly dealing theologically with the concerns of the parishioners. Often they create a bond of secrecy with an ally who can be counted on to protect the pastor if public scandal ever surfaces. This behavior is abusive.

The Needs of Parishioners

The complex theological mazes that clergy often construct for themselves in searching for answers and affirmations about God and humankind can be exceedingly disorienting to parishioners, and especially so at times of crisis. At such times it is better for a pastor to fall back on cliches of faith than to present the radical implications of the current line of theological reasoning the pastor is exploring personally. In some situations, responding with, "I don't know," or "It is a mystery," may be more helpful than a definitive, doctrinally correct pronouncement.

However, a pastor should not use this as an excuse to avoid using sound biblical scholarship in the pulpit and classroom. People are hungry for solid spiritual food. As long as the pastor speaks plainly, avoids arcane theological constructs, and is not inappropriately self-disclosing in the examples given, most parishioners are comfortable with, even encouraged by, the pastor's wrestling with scripture texts in preaching and teaching. But there are limits to how much spiritual angst any given congregation can take from its pastor.

Because they are vulnerable, parishioners in crisis need the quiet assurance and strength of mind of their pastors. Pastors who operate out of their personal doctrinal agendas can do the most harm by linking acceptance of their position with the continuation of care. That is, a subtle contract is established whereby the parishioner in need agrees to believe what the pastor pronounces in exchange for emotional support and attention. The counseling relationship in such a circumstance is not spiritually healthy because the pastor's motivation is furtherance of a theological agenda rather than the best interests of the parishioner. It is clearly a misuse of the pastoral office when a pastor uses a parishioner's crisis to prove some theological point to that parishioner (or worse yet, to other parishioners).

When pastors use their theological agendas or their appropriations of the doctrines of their traditions to control their parishioners, they are abusing the office of pastor and abusing the people they are sent to serve. When they use their superior knowledge of scripture to intimidate individuals, they are behaving like bullies. When they relate to people according to how willingly the people accept and support the pastors' views, they are committing clerical malpractice.

Operating out of theological agendas arises from the psychological needs of the pastors who act this way. Chapters 7 through 10 will address problems associated with these needs and offer suggestions for help. Ultimately, the needs of parishioners are best met by pastors who have worked through their neuroses, obsessions, low self-esteem, and so forth, and the second half of this book offers advice on how that can happen.

A Note about Sin

Although there are many nuances to theological positions on sin, in general, the conservative side of the spectrum focuses more energy on individual sin and personal morality, and the liberal side focuses more energy on corporate sin and systemic injustice. Conservatives use the tools of law and judgment to measure sin, while liberals use grace and justice for the same purpose.

In the context of pastoral care, the far ends of the spectrum—both conservative and liberal—can be harmful. A parishioner's guilt over personal sins may become morbid because of the overdramatized reaction of an extremely conservative pastor. On the other hand, a very liberal pastor may not take seriously the failings of a parishioner. A parishioner's guilt over some traumatic event or major misbehavior may be dismissed as insignificant by the liberal with a quick assurance of grace. Sometimes the liberal response may be even more dismissive by asserting that the guilt-inducing behavior is not sinful at all. Ultimately, it may not be sinful; nevertheless, it is problematic for the parishioner and needs to be taken seriously.

Confession and forgiveness are cornerstones of pastoral ministry, but individual church members need time to work through their feelings about their imperfect actions, and they need to accept appropriate personal responsibility for them. They cannot do this if they are frightened by pious and moralistic pronouncements or patronized with assurances of cheap grace. Law and grace must be held in tension and dispensed carefully in pastoral counseling situations.

One thing that conservatives, liberals, and all the rest have in common is a tendency to externalize evil. We all find sources of evil outside ourselves and outside the groups or institutions we belong to. I remember an adult Bible study class in a rural congregation. No matter what Bible passage was being studied on any given Sunday, the teacher managed to extract this message from it: We are blessed by God that we live out in the country in this good community instead of in that wicked city fifty miles away. The whole congregation reinforced this message by having no prayer of confession in the worship liturgy. The congregation was conservative, but liberal congregations are just as likely to create external scapegoats. This is a way to avoid examining or taking responsibility for one's own behavior, whether personal or group.

Pastors are as prone to this dynamic as congregations are. Sometimes pastors who know better are drawn into supporting their congregations in externalizing evil because helping them acknowledge their own unhealthy behavior is too hard. It is easier to acquiesce in the delusion than to work toward a balanced view of sin. Whatever a pastor's theology of sin may be, in pastoral care situations the best interests of parishioners must always be considered.

Someone dying from cirrhosis of the liver after years of alcohol abuse is not well served by a pastor who rails against the evils of drinking liquor or the sin of alcoholism. Neither is that person helped by a pastor who blames the disease on the machinations of nefarious purveyors of alcoholic beverages, glossing over the personal responsibility of the individual. Pastoral love, care, compassion, and acceptance flourish in an atmosphere of honesty that neither obsesses over nor denies the reality of sin.

Pastors in Jeopardy

If God ultimately judges all people by the consistency and objective correctness of their theological and doctrinal positions, then of all people, clergy stand in the greatest jeopardy. Given the incredible diversity of views and the splitting and resplitting of fine arguments to which clergy are prone, only a small number could possibly have hit on the exactly correct understanding of the nature and intentions of God.

If God judges people on the basis of simple faith and artless trust in the providence of God, then again, clergy are at grave risk because their theologizing tends to be sophisticated and conditional.

On the other hand, if God judges people on the extent to which they have appropriated to themselves knowledge of the will of God (the more the better), then clergy have a great chance for salvation, but heaven is likely to be sparsely populated. Perhaps the best pastors can do is to be true to their own beliefs while being well aware in all humility that in the end they may be wrong.

CHAPTER 6

Unrealistic Expectations

The Germans have a wonderful word for it: *aneinandervorbeireden.* It means "talking past one another," and that is what pastors and parishioners frequently do. Pastor and parishioner may speak the same language, but they mean different things with their words. They may observe the same event but have very different understandings of what they have seen. And much of the time they do not even know that they are operating out of different realities, so they believe they have communicated clearly when they have not. Thus, their expectations of each other are built on subjective assumptions about their different worlds.

The realm of parish ministry is crowded with unrealistic expectations from members of congregations and from pastors arising from their mutual misperceptions. The quality of ministry can be significantly affected by how pastors respond to these unrealistic expectations from their congregants, and even more so by how well pastors can recognize the extent of their own.

Here's a laundry list of common unrealistic expectations church members have of their pastors and pastors' families:

–The pastor agrees with my understanding of the faith.
–The pastor has no sexual feelings.
–The pastor likes children.
–The pastor is always kind and gentle.
–The pastor's sins, if any, are trivial and not as large as mine.
–The pastor's spouse likes singing in the choir and teaching in the church school.
–The pastor's children are always well behaved.

–The pastor's children love the church and believe in the church's
    doctrine just as the pastor does.
–The pastor knows everything in the Bible.
–The pastor is vitally interested in every detail of my life.

The list could go on for pages, but it would be useful for you to
create a list for reflection. Likewise, it would be good for you to think
about your expectations of your congregation that may be unrealistic.
What might they be?

Transference and Projection

Another dimension of unrealism from parishioners is the matter of transference. A parishioner may relate to a pastor in a particular way because
of the parishioner's experience with some other pastor in the past. For
example, a member may view the pastor as good and kind, even though
in reality the pastor may be brusque and uncaring, because the parishioner transfers to the pastor the previously experienced attributes of another pastor known in childhood.

Many pastors today enjoy free rides courtesy of the behavior of pastors several generations ago. Problems occur, however, when a parishioner has had a traumatic relationship with a pastor in childhood or at some
other vulnerable time. The current pastor may be feared or mistrusted
for the sins of another pastor.

Problems that arise because of transference usually must be dealt
with on an individual basis between the pastor and the parishioner. In
many cases the transference is harmless or works to the benefit of the
pastor and may as well be ignored or accepted graciously. But in cases
where transference causes serious tension or other problems in the
pastor-parishioner relationship, pastoral counseling from another pastor
(or in some cases a clinical therapist) may be warranted for parishioner
or pastor or both.

Akin to transference is the phenomenon of projection, which occurs
in negative and positive forms. Just as a pastor may receive unearned
credit or hostility from transference when a parishioner connects the
pastor with another person, the same may happen when a parishioner
projects self-feelings, either good or bad, onto the pastor.

Over the years a number of saintly parishioners have insistently described me as more kindly and good than I know to be true. They were, I believe, projecting their own spiritual goodness onto me as the identified representative of God. Other parishioners have seen in me evil intent that was not in me but in themselves. Negative projection is a lot harder to take. In any case, being alert to the possibility of projection may help pastors make sense of otherwise perplexing relationships with certain parishioners.

Unrealistic Expectations about Parishioners

The various tableaux of unrealistic expectations that parishioners create about their pastors tend to fade in benign fashion if the pastors are otherwise competent, effective, and well behaved. Pastors are more likely to have trouble with their own unrealistic expectations of their parishioners. The most common unrealistic expectation from pastors is that parishioners will respect them and follow their leads simply because they are pastors. That is, their status as clergy by itself is sufficient reason for people to obey them and grant them authority without having to earn it in any other way. This is an enticing misconception because frequently, parishioners grant pastors respect and authority based on the office they hold without regard to their performance—at least initially. This provisional deference contributes to the delusion that unearned respect will continue for as long as the pastor serves the congregation, regardless of where the pastor wants to lead them.

It will not. There are limits to how much respect and authority go with the clerical office, and different denominations have different levels of tolerance for unearned obedience. Every individual congregation has its limits, too. Hiding behind a clerical collar does not serve a congregation well, and ultimately, it harms the self-esteem of the pastor who does it. Regardless of denomination, pastors who recognize that they must earn the respect of their congregations and must demonstrate their competence to lead do far better in ministry than those who rely on the unrealistic expectation that the office will provide their authority.

A subtle and widespread unrealistic expectation among pastors is that the people in their congregations will change in response to their preaching or teaching. Over time, some people do change in response to pastors' messages–sermons, classes, funeral meditations, and so on. The number who do so within the time frame of any particular pastor's ministry is very small, however, and the degree to which they change is proportional to the level of crisis or trauma they have experienced coincidental with the pastor's tenure.

Sheer hubris leads pastors to believe that their carefully crafted words will cause people to change their behavior, alter what they believe, or convince them to turn their lives around. Pastors are merely agents of God, but even at that, they are not the only agents of God sowing seeds of change in the lives of people. A little humility would go a long way in this regard, and a significant lowering of expectations would bolster the self-esteem of pastors who become frustrated or disillusioned because no one seems to be changing in response to the deep and compelling sermons that they have delivered week after week.

Of course, words are their tools, so it is natural for pastors to expect that their words will have impact. And they will in tentative ways. On occasion parishioners may be moved to tears by the beauty of a pastor's words, but the effect will be evanescent. In the practical and materialistic culture of North America, what a pastor does is likely to be more influential in a congregation than what a pastor says. Spending one night in the waiting room of the critical care unit with the family of a parishioner who has suffered a massive heart attack speaks more powerfully than a dozen sermons, and it is remembered long after the elegant words of last week's sermon are consigned to unconscious oblivion.

It is also unrealistic for pastors to assume that all their parishioners are kindhearted people who always communicate in a straightforward and honest way. One of the least straightforward ways that many parishioners communicate is through gossip. People, pastors included, love to gossip. Gossip is exciting. It adds poetic interest to otherwise prosaic lives. Some of the best gossip centers on the activities of celebrities, and in any given neighborhood, town, or city, pastors are local celebrities. Therefore, pastors should expect a certain amount of behind-the-scenes talk about them and their families.

As long as the gossip is not mean-spirited, there is not much a pastor need do about it. If it is malicious, a pastor should seek assistance from denominational officials. In any case, however, the presence of gossip should be considered in context. More often than not, gossip would circulate about anyone serving as pastor. If it becomes a problem, it should be taken seriously but not personally.

A Note about Perfectionism

Some pastors are inclined to take much too personally the less-considerate behaviors of their parishioners, such as petty criticism or gossip. This leads me to the subject of perfectionism, for I refer here to perfectionists. A simplistic definition of a would be "a person who is highly motivated to do things perfectly all the time." The difficulty with this is that the pursuit of doing things well—as perfectly as possible—is a good thing. However, nuances to perfectionism create problems. A more complete definition would include that such a person has unrealistically high expectations for self, others, or both, coupled with a fear of making mistakes.

Perfectionists are very sensitive to criticism and gossip, overreacting to them and taking them personally rather than accepting these things in context. A perfectionist pastor tends to be an all-or-nothing thinker. A sermon, for example, is either a great success or a dismal failure. If it is not perfect, it is not worth anything. A few words of constructive criticism from a parishioner will send a perfectionist pastor into a tizzy of self-reproach for having produced such a poor sermon. If the perfectionism is extreme, the pastor would go so far as to rewrite the sermon to perfect it, even though it would never be delivered again.

Perfectionism arises, I believe, from the waters of chaos, from childhoods without reliable limits. All the perfectionist pastors I know grew up in families in which their parents either set no particular boundaries or the norms of family life were mostly unspoken, yet they were punished or humiliated by their parents if they did something wrong. Perfectionists learn during childhood how to make rules for themselves to avoid the negative consequences of making mistakes. And the first rule of perfectionism is: "I should have known better." Following this rule prevents perfectionists from forgiving themselves for any mistake, misstep, or miscalculation.

Perfectionist pastors are usually quite good at performing the tasks of ministry. They work hard to do these things right in order to compensate for the parts of their lives they cannot control. But some may become compulsive about the activities at which they excel and avoid ones at which they are only adequate, lest their imperfections become commonly known.

The unsupervised world of parish ministry, with its peculiar norms for each congregation (spoken and unspoken), is an enticing environment for perfectionists because they know how to take responsibility for other people's irresponsibility. They learned in childhood how to thrive in households with movable, often invisible boundaries, so they experience a comfortable familiarity with similar dynamics in parish ministry. If anything goes wrong, they blame themselves first, perhaps concluding that the parishioners deserve better than their bungling efforts. Parishioners seldom challenge this behavior regardless of the source of the irregularity because it relieves them of their own pain.

Perfectionist pastors are prime candidates for burnout because of the high level of energy required to do nearly everything perfectly all the time. They are prone, also, to carrying the burden of responsibility for the complete emotional and spiritual health of their parishioners. They believe that all the things they do or fail to do have serious consequences affecting the lives of their congregants. Therefore, they cannot rest until every last detail is covered. Not only does this overfunctioning harm the pastors themselves, but it is also disastrous for parishioners because it leads to congregational dependence and underfunctioning. The extraordinary efforts of the perfectionist pastor weaken the ability of the membership to do its rightful ministry.

The most grievous aspect of perfectionism for pastors is that they are reluctant to accept forgiveness and grace for themselves. They may be very good at reassuring parishioners, but for themselves, well, they should have known better. Ironically, this is another unrealistic expectation, that God's grace extends to everyone else but somehow has a warp in it that leaves the perfectionist uncovered.

Despite its all-or-nothing thinking pattern, perfectionism is not an all-or-nothing condition. It can be present in varying shades of intensity and more pronounced in some situations than in others. It can wax and wane many times over a lifetime. If you identify perfectionist tendencies in yourself and you want to work on the problem, you may respond well to supervision from a nonanxious, gentle, boundary-setting mentor. Look around for a colleague who fits that description and ask for help.

Depression

There are among us pastors who (at least in public) are perpetually smiling. Everything is always beautiful. In private, however, even the most persistent optimist will acknowledge that life in parish ministry is not always beautiful. And it is unrealistic for pastors to expect that things will always go well in the pastorate. Further, it is unrealistic for pastors to assume they will be able to handle at all times everything that comes along. Whether it be in response to painful episodes or spiritually draining times or other factors, many pastors suffer bouts of depression. Indeed, so widespread is this phenomenon that I have come to think of depression as the pastors' disease. Those who escape it are the fortunate minority among clergy.

The first thing a pastor suffering depression needs to know is that there is no shame in it. It is a sign of humanness but not a sign of failure. The second thing is that you're among good company and there is no reason to suffer silently and alone. You may be able to deal with temporary bouts of depression by talking with a friend or colleague. Prolonged or profound depressions require professional help from a psychologist or psychiatrist.

If depression comes, take it seriously, but don't be afraid of it. Seek an appropriate level of help. If going to a friend doesn't bring relief, take the next step by finding a counselor or therapist. If you heed medication or hospitalization, a therapist should be able to refer you to suitable medical providers. With time and proper treatment, depression will lift and life will seem good again.

Volunteers and Amateurs

Virtually all pastors enter ministry with high levels of commitment to their churches. Usually, their commitments are greater in time and energy than their parishioners are willing or able to make.[1] On the other hand, most pastors are paid comfortable salaries that allow them the luxury of such commitments. Pastors who expect from parishioners a level of commitment to the church equal to their own are setting themselves up for disappointment. It is unrealistic to expect volunteers, which church members essentially are, to devote the same time and energy to the enterprise of the church that pastors do. Some few church members will come close, for a variety of reasons, not all of them noble. For the most part, however, parishioners are amateurs, in the original sense of the word, which means that they are lovers. They come to church because they are drawn there, trying to love God through the discipline of worship. Let that be the base level expectation, and anything beyond that becomes a wondrous gift.

If persisted in, unrealistic expectations held by pastors can undermine ministry. Well-adjusted pastors recognize their own limits and do not overemphasize their importance or the effect of their work on people they serve.

CHAPTER 7

Codependence

Even well-ordered, well-to-do congregations may have a few crazy folk among the members. Religious organizations seem to attract a disproportionately large share of the world's maladjusted people. This only makes sense because virtually all religious organizations define themselves in terms of openness to any who would believe the teachings of that organization, regardless of any other factors.

In actual practice, some congregations are very good at subtly or even overtly excluding certain people from their membership. Poverty, race, social status, education, marital status, native language, and physical handicap all have been factors used to exclude people from participation in church activities. Mental health, however, has not been widely used as a criterion for membership.

People who are well adjusted socially, with well-integrated minds, and who enjoy good mental health sit side by side in the pews with people who are antisocial misfits, even sociopaths. Well-mannered members sit around tables in church board meetings with boors. Lay leaders who work cooperatively with pastors to accomplish good works have among them other lay leaders who are uncooperative and obstructive in their behavior. Committee members who function openly and honestly share their tasks with people who seek to manipulate and control the committee processes.

These mentally unhealthy or maladjusted people may be few in number in any given congregation (although some congregations seem to attract them in greater numbers than others), but they tend to wield influence well beyond their numbers. Only one or two disturbed people on a church board may undermine the mission of the congregation and render ineffective the leadership of the pastor. Mentally healthy people want to be kind, considerate, and loving, and in North American church culture, that means not confronting the troublemakers unless they become physically abusive, and then only if they act out in public.

I have seen church boards paralyzed by the manipulations of one alcoholic member, the malignant mouthings of a single bigot, or the cajoling of a charismatic sociopath. I have seen congregations held hostage to the extremist views of one family. I have seen mission funding for congregations undermined by misanthropic treasurers who balked at writing checks for expenditures they did not like. And I have seen churches protect and support the mentally sickest among them, all in the name of love and charity.

To make matters worse, pastors tend to be in the vanguard of supporters of these maladjusted parishioners. It is not surprising that pastors want to be liked by their parishioners, and many pastors have the strong need to please other people. Even if some of the people are making their lives miserable and their jobs impossible, pastors work hard to be nice to the ones who are most responsible for their pastoral misery. They cave in to the unreasonable demands of the sociopath. They make excuses for the bizarre behavior of the alcoholic. They allow their boards to wallow in indecision to assuage the fears of the neurotic. They appease the bigot and defer to the fanatic.

These pastors are codependents. They are no different from the spouse who supports and protects an alcoholic mate. They are no different from the wife who is beaten by her husband year after year without getting help and without reporting the abuse to authorities. They are no different from the husband who is repeatedly demeaned and degraded verbally by a vitriolic wife and who passively accepts the calumny without complaint. They are no different from any other human beings who feel deep down that they deserve the abuse because of their own lack of worth.

Codependence is a wild epidemic in religious institutions today, and pastors are the primary carriers of the disease. Pastors bear major responsibility for codependent functioning because they are officially or de facto the leaders in their congregations. A church board with codependent (or otherwise dysfunctional) members cannot move beyond its effective paralysis if the pastor is also codependent. Confident and competent leadership from the pastor is required for an unhealthy board to work toward healthy functioning.

Even in a case where most of the board members are well-functioning people, but the pastor is codependent and continues to enable the few malfunctioning members to cast their distorted shadows over the whole group, the healthy ones probably will not be able to transcend the pathology of the organization. Instead, the most likely option for the healthy folk in this scenario is to focus on the deficiencies of the pastor, seeking either to remedy them or to get rid of the pastor, even if the pastor's dysfunction is considerably less than that of the troubled board members. Leadership is crucial to the success of any organization and minor flaws in a leader are more significant than major flaws in followers.

At this point I frequently enter the scene as pastor to pastors. And the greatest challenge I face in these situations is to avoid becoming codependent myself. Since my job is to support and advocate for pastors in trouble, the temptation to prop up incompetent pastors and cover up for malpracticing ones is ever present. On occasion, I confess, I have succumbed to temptation. Some days I feel that my job is to patch up wounded pastors just enough to send them back into their congregational arenas, knowing the patches will not hold. A certain amount of codependence seems to be built in to the structure of ministry, whether it be a pastor protecting a parishioner or a denominational official covering for a pastor. But in the long run this ecclesiastical codependence does no one any good.

Compared with confronting problem pastors with the unpleasant reality of their situations, my experience is that supporting these pastors against their congregations or governing bodies is the easier task, even when doing so is clearly codependent and harmful to the congregation. Congregations expect governing bodies to protect the pastor, and governing bodies tend to have a great deal of softness surrounding their discipline. Reproving pastors with tough love—playing the Dutch uncle—is the more difficult task. Following the disciplined approach and avoiding codependence, I have encountered animosity—even hostility—from wayward pastors who expected unqualified support and sympathy from *their* pastor. Speaking the truth in love is not popular with the ones who must listen to it. This expectation that the pastor to pastors should cover and protect colleagues from the consequences of their unproductive behavior creates a tension in the position that has yet to be resolved.

Enabling: Type 1

Fashionable these days in denominational contexts is the word *enabler*.
Pastors point with pride to their enabling styles of leadership. In the
world of twelve-step programs for recovering addicts and in psychotherapy circles, however, an enabler is not a good thing to be.

In churchspeak, enablers are pastors who help parishioners learn to
conduct the ministry of the church for themselves. This is enabling type
1. The concept is a useful one, but in practice it often fails. One reason
is that many church members, especially in small churches, interpret the
pastor's teaching them to do the work of the church as pastoral laziness.
That is, the pastor is enabling them to do what the pastor does not want
to do. They are not always wrong in this interpretation, for busy pastors
are often tempted to encourage parishioners to handle the pastoral tasks
they like least or are least skilled at. This hearkens back to the chapter
dealing with paying dues. If church members perceive these transferred
tasks as key pastoral activities, the pastor may be answered with resentment for enabling parishioners to do them.

In such cases, pastors need to be honest with their boards about their
strengths and weaknesses and work out plans for ministry that reflect the
variety of gifts available in the congregation. Even then, pastors must
perform some tasks whether or not they like doing them. Many pastors,
for example, find taking Communion to homebound members painful.
Several pastors I know have tried to find ways to have board members
do this ministry without the pastor participating. Apart from doctrinal or
polity requirements, parish dynamics make this kind of enabling counter-
productive. Pastors who see themselves as enablers need to monitor their
work to ensure that they are faithfully encouraging the ministry of the
laity and not inviting their boards into codependent relationships with
them.

Enabling: Type 2

For some codependent pastors, an underlying problem is the inability to
discern what is rightfully the pastor's responsibility and what belongs to
the board or congregation. In theory, enabling pastors would provide
encouragement and counsel to board members to solve church problems

but would not try to solve the problems for them. If they actually functioned this way, great things could happen, but too few pastors do.

The more common form of enabling in congregations is type 2, the twelve-step kind. In the guise of caring for people, codependent pastors enable them to remain dysfunctional. The codependent enabling pastor works hard to solve other people's problems. When this is not possible, the enabler accepts responsibility for the decisions and actions of others, regardless of how ill-conceived and rash they may be.

Codependent enabling pastors frequently garner great praise from parishioners for taking care of them so well, but that praise is little consolation when the inevitable burnout and breakdown ignominiously truncate promising careers. Being in a codependent relationship with one other person takes a toll, but consider the emotional stress and physical consequences of being codependent with an entire congregation. This is what codependent pastors have at stake.

A Note about Triangulation

Dialogue, a decade or so ago, was a buzzword in church circles. Pastors were intent on being in dialogue with everyone about every conceivable problem or issue. In many church situations, however, direct conversation between people has not been the primary form of communication. Typically, triangulation is favored over dialogue, especially when the subject is disagreeable. Triangulation is certainly a favorite method for codependents to communicate, but it is not exclusively a codependent phenomenon.

Parishioners and pastors frequently communicate with each other via triangulation. Someone wants to affect, influence, or pass information on to someone else but does not want to do so directly. Therefore, a third party is used as intermediary, forming a triangle. Triangulated intermediaries are notoriously poor conductors of information or influence; nevertheless, the practice continues unabated, with tragicomic results.

Here is an example of triangulation in a congregation: Uncle Bo has been brooding about his mortality and wants the pastor to call on him at home so he can discuss his thoughts. However, he is somewhat embarrassed about the matter and does not want the pastor to know that he is worried about it. He wants to slip it into a conversation casually. Therefore, he does not want to initiate a request for a pastoral visit because if he did, the pastor might ask whether something was wrong. Not only that, he has it in his mind that if he has to ask the pastor to visit, it does not count for much.

Uncle Bo wants the pastor somehow to intuit that he needs a visit and come by without being asked. Not being an intuitive person himself, however, Uncle Bo feels the need to prod the pastor's intuition just a little, so he tells a member of the church board that some day—no hurry, mind you—it would be nice if the pastor would pay him a call at home.

Several things could result from this triangulated communication. One is that the board member may conclude that the pastor is not visiting church members. The board member may say nothing at all to the pastor or may suggest that the pastor visit more members without mentioning Uncle Bo by name. A very sensitive board member may infer from Uncle Bo's comment that Uncle Bo is seriously ill and may approach the pastor in a dramatic panic. In any case, the likelihood is low that Uncle Bo's triangulation will accomplish what he wants, which is simply for the board member to tell the pastor to visit him without making a fuss about it.

This example is relatively harmless, but all too often pastors are hit broadside by the triangulated conversations of angry parishioners who do not have the self-confidence or courage to speak to them face-to-face. Third parties frequently convey complaints, gossip, rumors, hurt feelings, misunderstandings, and disagreements to pastors, thus creating triangles of unhappy parishioners, reluctant or unwitting messengers, and dismayed pastors.

Expecting parishioners to communicate directly all the time may be unrealistic, but pastors can improve the level of communication by de-triangulating whenever possible. Pastors can refuse in some situations to be drawn into intermediary communication by identifying the triangulation to the messenger. They can also refrain from triangulating. Uncle Bo's example notwithstanding, pastors are tempted to triangulate at least as much as parishioners, with similar results. Even if they cannot control other people doing this, pastors can exercise self-control by communicating directly with people with whom they need to talk. Some parishioners will respond in kind, and this is all to the good.

Here is a cautionary comment about pastoral triangulation. Pastors have traditionally triangulated with parishioners through their spouses. Information, concerns, complaints, defensive explanations, and gossip a pastor wants to reach certain people but feels constrained to say directly can be disseminated through the spouse to certain supportive friends in the congregation. Using a spouse to triangulate happens far too often, and it is always unwise. Pastors who are tempted to communicate this way need to consider their motives for doing it.

Three Things to Help

What, then, can a codependent pastor do to get beyond this dysfunction? An easy but entirely unrealistic answer is to stop being nice to difficult people. But a pastor cannot do this because being nice is part of the job description. It is one of the major role expectations of clergy in North American culture. Regardless of how curt or critical parishioners may be with one another, the pastor is counted on to be the resident nice person, the representative of the kindness of God. Straying too far from this norm is sure grounds for a troubled pastorate.

Of course, there are ways of being nice to people without accepting or enabling their pathological behavior. Unfortunately, for many co-dependents the nuances of effective human interaction have been blotted out in earlier stages of life, and they are not able to see, much less set, clear boundaries.

Three things that can be helpful for codependent pastors are pastors' support groups, leadership training seminars, and therapy (especially group therapy with other codependents).

Support groups provide encouragement and understanding from peers who experience the same kinds of problems in their parishes. Many kinds of pastors' support groups exist, from essentially social gatherings to self-selected groups who covenant to work on significant personal issues. Some are exclusively male or female, some cross de-nominational lines, and some are maintained across great geographical distances. A good source for information on pastors' support groups is Roy M. Oswald's book *How to Build a Support System for Your Ministry*, published by The Alban Institute.[1]

Here is an idea for a self-identified codependent pastor who would like to be in a pastors' support group in an area where none exists or where no existing one would be appropriate or comfortable. Try taking the risk of getting a group started with a few selected people. It may not work out, but succeed or fail, it would be good practice in demonstrating leadership. And since a pastors' support group operates beyond the parish, even if the group falls flat, there will be no negative consequences to deal with from congregants.

This leads to the middle suggestion above, leadership training seminars. These have become a great industry over the last decade or so, and many are available even in remote areas. Most of them are focused on business or political leadership, but the underlying principles can be used in any setting, including ministry, with only minor adaptations. Leadership education is important for codependent pastors because deficient or defective leadership skills and codependent behavior are frequently wrapped together in the same human package.

Face-to-face leadership training events are, of course, more effective, for they provide opportunities to practice what is taught and to interact with the teachers. Where such seminars are not financially or geographically accessible, however, a secondary source of help is the plethora of books, tapes, and videos available for moderate cost through mail order or free through local libraries.

The third suggestion for dealing with codependence is therapy. Support groups and leadership education can build confidence and improve effectiveness in dealing with people, but if the underlying causes of codependence are not dealt with, the newly acquired confidence will quickly collapse for lack of a firm foundation. Codependent behavior has roots in previous life experience. The roots need to be examined, cleaned, replanted, and nurtured. If for no other reason than they provide counseling to troubled parishioners, pastors need to experience therapy for themselves. If a tendency toward codependence is also present and recognized, a pastor needs to go directly to therapy without delay. Rather than indicate failure and punishment, therapy represents the opening door to freedom and success in ministry. These three things can help a codependent pastor become well equipped for effective parish leadership.

CHAPTER 8

Addictions

Well-versed professionals frequently make distinctions among addiction, compulsion, and obsession. In recent years, however, the criteria separating them have become blurred, and the term *addiction* has been used widely to include more than substance addiction (e. g., alcohol or drugs). Certain behaviors are now commonly called addictions, and I use this broader sense of the term here.

Forty-five minutes ago I learned that my cousin, who had recently completed a rehabilitation program for alcoholism, was found dead at his home this morning, apparently from liver disease. He was in his midforties. Five minutes ago I got off the phone with an attorney after clarifying with him some details relating to yet another pastor who has been acting out sexually with parishioners. How these experiences will affect what follows, I do not know, but this is acknowledgment that I am grieving as I write.

Using the term *addiction* broadly, I am aware that a majority of the clergy I have known are either codependent or addicted (or both). This rather sweeping statement encompasses a wide spectrum of intensities and toxicities of addiction. That is, some may be mildly addicted to exercise, which has a beneficial effect (but has a potentially harmful side to it), while others may be completely out of control with addiction to alcohol, which is rapidly poisoning their bodies and impairing their judgment. Whatever a person is addicted to becomes a kind of medication to ease the pain of life in order to avoid living with and through that pain. As I write this, I have just eaten six chocolate chip cookies, even though I am not hungry. I could sit here and eat the whole package to assuage the pain of my grief, but I have put the package away because I owe it to my cousin to mourn for him and I owe it to myself to refrain from abusing my body.

Much has been written about addiction to alcohol and other drugs by people with a great deal more knowledge and insight than I possess. Though there are clergy who are substance abusers, I would refer them to professional therapists and to Alcoholics Anonymous or Narcotics Anonymous for help. This is not a self-help book for addicts. My goal for this chapter is to raise the subject in such a way that you who read these words will engage in some self-reflection and self-assessment about your possible addictions.

Here is a list of behaviors associated with addictions, all of which I have observed among clergy:

—Lying repeatedly, especially about small matters
—Claiming credit for work done by others
—Covering mistakes by blaming others
—Operating in secrecy
—Having frequent suspicions of others' actions
—Feeling persecuted by parishioners or denominational officials
—Experiencing difficulty in describing actual events consistent with how others describe them
—Being unable to make even minor decisions
—Lacking dependability in following through on tasks once agreed upon
—Having frequent unaccounted-for absences during the working day

This list is not exhaustive. There are many more indicators of possible addiction, and any of them may apply to people who are not addicts. Nevertheless, these behaviors are common among clergy, and the list is a starting point for personal contemplation. As a spiritual exercise, you could reform each item on the list into a question and meditate on the matter. For example, you could ask yourself, "Do I lie repeatedly about small matters?"

The most common addictions I have encountered among parishioners during my years as a pastor are (in alphabetical order) alcohol, drugs, food, gossip, reading for escape, sex, and tobacco. Except for tobacco, which is comparatively less common among pastors, these same addictions occur among clergy, I would guess, with about the same frequency as among parishioners. Pastors who suspect they may be addicted to any of these can find a great deal of literature in any chain bookstore that will help them evaluate their situations.

Sex Addiction

Sex addiction is a complex subject with many nuances requiring specialized attention beyond the scope of this book. Still, some comments about sexual acting out are appropriate here. Pastors who engage in sexual relations with parishioners are not necessarily sex addicts, but the number of pastors who improperly cross sexual boundaries is not small, and some level of therapeutic intervention is needed when it happens. Rather than sex, some other addiction, such as power, may be involved, or something other than an addictive process may be at work.

. My observation is that pastors who act out in sexual ways tend to be very bright, creative, and energetic. Physical attractiveness does not play much of a role, but charisma does, as well as authoritarian personality. That is, those with highly magnetic personalities and those with authoritarian bents seem to be at higher risk for this behavior. Also, those with well-developed imaginations can be tempted to act on their fantasies if opportunities arise (as inevitably they do in parish settings). Pastors who recognize in themselves some risk toward sexual misadventure would be wise to seek counseling before they get caught up in activities that would end their careers.

Holding to theological beliefs that condemn sexual activity outside marriage does not seem to provide a significant defense in preventing this behavior, regardless of whether it is an addictive process. Pastors who identify themselves as orthodox, traditional, conservative, evangelical, charismatic, progressive, liberal, or any other label are equally liable to engage in sexual misconduct.

In years past, unless a public scandal erupted, pastors who had engaged in sexual relations with parishioners often were moved quietly to another parish. Today, because of changes in the larger society, in particular the increasing political clout of women and the growth in litigiousness, this behind-the-scenes maneuvering is rarely possible. Threats of lawsuits have made denominational officers wary of ignoring any accusations of sexual harassment or misconduct, however tentative they may be. Several denominations have developed sexual misconduct

screening systems to protect congregations from offenders who try to
move to other parishes.

Current conversation about pastors involved sexually with parishioners focuses on power dynamics. Since the great majority of these cases
involve male pastors, much has been made of the power advantages that
male pastors possess in dealing with parishioners and female colleagues.
Most of the time when sexual misconduct occurs, this power analysis
holds true, and it can be very helpful for victims of sexual abuse to recognize that they had little or no control over the situation in the midst
of the sexual activity.

However, pastors who are sex addicts need some form of therapy
dealing with the addictive process before acknowledgment of the abuse
of the power inherent in their offices and gender can have much effect.
When confronted, pastors who are sexually predatory, that is, those who
are the worst abusers, are usually the last to acknowledge their misuse of
power, while those who strayed once in the midst of personal crisis generally accept readily that they have abused their personal power. Some
of them even become excessively remorseful and assume the guilt that
the persistent abusers refuse to accept.

The abuse of power model is problematic for another group of pastors. Some pastors have poor decision-making skills when it comes to
personal relationships, especially intimate ones. Commonly, this inability to make good choices has origins in childhood and is fueled by low
self-esteem. Such pastors may have impaired abilities to resist being
exploited personally and can be drawn into or even initiate sexual situations that they know to be wrong but feel powerless to avoid. The power perspective recognizes low self-esteem among women as a factor that
undercuts any interpersonal power they would otherwise have. Having
low self-esteem would make it difficult, for example, for a female pastor
to resist the advances from a male colleague.

My experience reveals, however, that low self-esteem among pastors
is not an exclusively female phenomenon. Although others may perceive
male pastors as powerful, those with low self-esteem do not feel powerful. A small number of pastors—male and female—who become sexually involved with parishioners are acting out of feelings of powerlessness and thus may not respond beneficially to education or therapy that
focuses on their abuse of power. A sense of powerlessness—inability to
resist temptation—has associations with addiction, so the matter comes

full circle. Some kind of addiction or codependent process may be involved when pastors with low self-esteem act out sexually.

For pastors who have acted out sexually but are not habitual abusers, a model emphasizing pastors' personal responsibility may be more helpful than one focusing on the abuse of power since these pastors generally respond positively to intervention. On the other hand, the greatest benefit from the abuse of power model is prevention, and thus it needs to be broadly disseminated. With proper education, pastors who may be at risk for sexual misconduct can use this knowledge as an early warning device to monitor their behavior and avoid potentially dangerous situations.

Work Addiction

An addiction I have observed among parishioners but I have seen with greater frequency among clergy is work. Some days it seems redundant to say a particular pastor is a workaholic because too often workaholism is tacitly understood to be a prerequisite for ordination. But then I remember that there are distinctions between hard work for long hours and workaholism. One difference is that the workaholic, for all the long hours devoted to work, seldom produces consistent, quality work or gets caught up. The workaholic tends to make a lot of mistakes and thus spends time redoing things. Another distinction is that the workaholic does not voluntarily take breaks or get needed rest. Addiction to work is addiction to stress, which leads to burnout or premature death.

Workaholics harm themselves and others by caving in to the persistent urge to do something, take action, or control events when the opposite is needed. Workaholics are reluctant to let matters unfold naturally, so they rush in to fill the perceived void of inactivity with anything that will keep themselves busy and events churning.

As a result, problems often grow larger because workaholics cannot leave them alone. Situations get worse because of irritation from their constant tinkering, from forcing premature activity, or from spending too much time with small matters, thereby granting them greater importance.

The expression "if it ain't broke, don't fix it" is anathema to some workaholics. I have seen them sabotage projects just as they are about to be completed so that they could continue working on them. Almost always, however, they are unaware that they have done so. "If it is fixed, break it" may be the unconscious motto of workaholics.

Practicing patience and spiritual exercises focusing on being rather than doing may be beneficial for recovering workaholics. Before jumping into this, however, the first step in recovery is getting a complete physical examination to assess the damage stress has already done. Attending Workaholics Anonymous is the next step.

Computer Addiction

This newcomer among addictions is a genuine twentieth-century phenomenon: computers. Although I have never encountered the word *computerholic*, perhaps it is now needed. Clergy, especially those born during or after World War II, have in large numbers enthusiastically taken up the computer as a tool for ministry. Some of them have become addicted to using their computers.

The world of personal computers is one where the operator makes commands that are followed instantaneously, creating whatever fantasy the operator wishes. It is a safe world in which difficult parishioners do not demand attention. In fact, difficult parishioners can be consigned to oblivion in the make-believe world of computers. Much important work can be done efficiently with a computer—weekly bulletins, sermons, letters, financial statements, and so on—but lots of beguiling yet frivolous things can be done, also.

The computerholic will inevitably find more things to be done via computer than need to be done for the well-being of the parish. The computerholic will find vast projects to produce on the computer that somehow crowd out the time needed to visit parishioners. The computerholic will count as golden the hours spent at the keyboard and will allow the hours to increase gradually while the hours devoted to face-to-face ministry with parishioners decrease. And all the while the computerholic will believe that the time spent with the computer is work for the benefit of the congregation.

Another dimension to computer pathology can be found in churches with large staffs or large physical plants. Some churches are extensively equipped with computer stations so that all staff members are able to communicate with one another via their computer terminals. Busy pastors and other church professionals can benefit from leaving messages quickly and efficiently as they rush from one meeting or pastoral emergency to another. However, the potential is here for abuse if the staff members begin to develop relationships and styles of communication that are shaped by the computer more than by personal interaction with one another. If there is any institution left on earth in which direct human conversation should be the highest priority, it is the Church. Consider the New Revised Standard Version translation of 3 John, verses 13-14: "I have much to write to you, but I would rather not write with pen and ink; instead I hope to see you soon, and we will talk together face to face." If he were writing today, I suspect that John would replace pen and ink with computer keyboard. Where computer addiction creeps in, talking together face-to-face decreases.

Gossip Addiction

However, another form of talking face-to-face (or via telephone) is problematic. Pastors who are addicted to gossip can produce great harm in their ministries. In chapter 6 I discussed parishioners gossiping about pastors. Some amount of public talk about the pastor is inevitable because of the high visibility of the position, and for the most part it is not harmful. But the reverse is not true. Pastors must exercise caution and discretion when it comes to talking to anyone else about parishioners or colleagues. At what point straightforward conversation becomes gossip is difficult to say, although most pastors are able to identify the difference between the two in particular situations.

Pastors addicted to gossip have little or no sense of judicious boundaries in their conversations. A gossip addict has a strong urge to know what's going on in people's lives combined with an even greater need to pass this information on to others. A temporary sense of being in the know—of informational power—is gained from passing colorful tidbits to others. This satisfaction is transitory and can be reexperienced only by gathering and transmitting more gossip.

The great temptation for pastors who are addicted to gossip is to invade their body of pastoral confidences when no other information is available. Some change details of pastoral counseling situations and reveal them in sermons. Others do it less publicly but no less destructively by describing such "disguised" matters to selected church officers or members. It rarely takes much effort for parishioners to figure out the real subject in these cases. Of course, the sense of betrayal felt by an exposed counselee is profound and the anger prolonged.

Pastors who gossip explicitly, identifying parishioners by name, are clearly in the realm of clerical malpractice and are exposing themselves and their denominations to lawsuits. Short of that, however, when parishioners come to believe they can no longer trust their pastor with the details of their personal lives, that ministry is effectively over, regardless of how much longer the pastor stays in the parish.

Audience Addiction

Another phenomenon found among clergy is addiction to audience. Some are drawn to the pulpit out of the need to be heard. Those who are addicted to audience get high from the performance. They need to be in the spotlight, and they will do anything to become the center of attention. Addicts prepare and deliver their sermons in ways that will get the greatest response from their congregations. Conveying the message of the sermon is not nearly as important as manipulating the hearers to emotional responses.

Positive feedback is the nectar that audience addicts crave, and they will shape their words to elicit the greatest positive response, even at the expense of the integrity of their religious beliefs. They need the fix that only a group of admiring listeners can provide, and they will say anything to get it.

It can be a subtle addiction, which is probably almost universal among pastors at a low level of intensity. Most pastors consider the effect of their words on their parishioners, and they are tempted to prepare their messages for maximum impact. Good preaching requires that sermons be prepared and delivered in ways that will engage the people where they are, capture their imaginations, touch their hearts. But things get distorted when pastors begin to rely on the positive feedback of parishioners and produce sermons that pander to the prejudices of congregations rather than ponder the mysteries of the faith.

Power, Doctrine, and Danger Addictions

Other addictions found among clergy are power, doctrine, and danger. Often power and doctrine are dual addictions wrapped around each other. The addictive process is present when being in control over people or giving them orders produces a satisfying glow that does not happen when simply cooperating with people in a common endeavor. Addiction may also be operating when a pastor needs to be the sole source of doctrinal information or interpretation for a congregation or the filter through which all doctrinal or theological questions are pressed.

People who have the need to be the expert, to have the right answers, to be the keepers of orthodoxy, to be authorities, and to have authority within their traditions are strongly drawn to careers in ministry. To what extent such people are addicted to power or doctrine, however, is open to evaluation in each case because other factors such as narcissism, sociopathy, and low self-esteem may be responsible.

Perhaps the adrenaline rush from being in peril is responsible for the danger addiction. A few pastors thrive on the edges of parish life, taking pride in taking positions that will surely get them in trouble with their congregations. They call themselves prophets and perform provocative deeds designed to gain them condemnation. This is different from truly prophetic speech or action, for the motivation with the danger addict is the high that comes from the behavior, not the value of the message or deed.

Another form of danger addiction is achieving a high that comes from almost being caught in compromising positions. Some pastors work just beyond the borders of propriety in personal relationships, savoring the narrow escapes from being discovered, for example, in an embrace with a member of the congregation. Of course, this could be considered a form of sex addiction.

A Note about Congregational Growth and Decline

In each of the parishes I served, I made a point of visiting inactive members and listening carefully to their stories. Over time, as I became more comfortable hearing horror stories about the church, visiting inactives came to be one of my favorite pastoral activities. The common lore about inactive members is that they are problem makers, difficult to get along with, quick to abandon commitments, emotionally troubled, spiritually shallow, or fickle. Yes, some of them are. For the majority, however, the opposite seems to be true. Some of the most thoughtful, spiritually astute, sensitive, gentle people I have ever met were inactive church members.

In any given congregation, certain people will drift away from active participation for a variety of motives. Usually, they depart quietly. In congregations characterized by addiction or codependence, a significant proportion of the inactives will be the mentally healthiest and spiritually most mature people in the congregation. To avoid being caught up in sick systems, they absent themselves. They drop out to save themselves, regardless of the source of dysfunction. That is, healthy people leave their congregations when their pastors are addicts or codependents and also when significant numbers of board members and other lay leaders are addicts or codependents.

This phenomenon has major implications for membership growth and decline. Congregations dominated by addicts or codependents consistently lose many of their best and brightest members out the back door of inactivity. They also quickly lose many of the inquiring souls who come in the front door. The least healthy are inclined to stay and the rest to drift away. Especially in small congregations, new members have much difficulty integrating into congregational life if the congregation functions as an addictive/codependent system. Much time and effort are needed for codependent members to cover for addicted pastors or for codependent pastors to protect dysfunctional board members. This activity leaves little time for productive ministry.

No denominational evangelism program has a chance of succeeding while enormous amounts of pastoral and congregational energy are channeled into addictive or codependent behavior. A bad news system cannot proclaim good news with authenticity, and only those who are comfortable with bad news (codependents) and those with well-honed denial skills will tolerate for very long a dysfunctional or dishonest system in a voluntary organization like a church.

Many volumes have been written about the membership decline in long-established denominations. Various good reasons have been advanced for this phenomenon, but curiously lacking in most of the reports has been any acknowledgment that far too many congregations and denominational organizations are stuck in the grip of addictive and codependent pathology. In a sense, these denominations are pushing out their healthy members so the sick ones can tend themselves.

Magnetic People, Places, and Things

The world is magnetic, and we humans are continually attracted to so very many people, places, and things, even though there is no possible way we can ever visit, touch, or respond to all of them. So we must make choices. Another way of saying this is that we must commit ourselves to a limited number of relationships, communities, and institutions to which we discern the most pressing calls, and for the sake of our commitments, we must let go of the rest, no matter how beguiling they may be. We must also try to discern which calls will produce the greatest good and which may be destructive.

Addicts have great difficulty with the unending possibilities that they are drawn to but can't have, so either they burn themselves out trying to reach everywhere and everything or they cover their grief by losing themselves in their addictions. One of the toughest obstacles recovering addicts have to surmount is figuring out how to live with the longing for all the beautiful, magnetic people, places, and things.

To be faithful to the beautiful call you have responded to as a pastor, addict or not, you need to accept the aching reality that as a consequence of that choice, there are many other beautiful things that you cannot do or have. Undoubtedly, some places in your heart will remain unrequited as long as you live. When you respond to one place, you must relinquish others. When you commit to one particular relationship, you must let go of others.

One of the ways you can be most helpful to your parishioners is by modeling for them a healthy life of commitment and relinquishment, showing them how to live with the ache. This is something that an actively addicted pastor cannot do, but it is something that a pastor recovering from addictions may be able to do with magnetic authenticity.

Therapy and Twelve-Step Programs

Any thing, behavior, or experience can be addicting, including devotional and religious activities. The addictions noted above are only a sampling of what clergy are subject to. Substances or behaviors that offer temporary release from pain or pleasant feelings are not necessarily bad, but they become problematic when you lose control and duplicating the experience, repeating the high, and covering the pain become primary motivators in your life.

What can you do if you suspect addiction? The answer is the same one that you would give a parishioner. Find a therapist and join a twelve-step program. Alcoholics Anonymous is the best known twelve-step program, but there are dozens of others, including Overeaters Anonymous, Workaholics Anonymous, Gamblers Anonymous, and so on.

In many cities, information about twelve-step meetings is available from the local Contact Help Line or similar agency. Telephone directories in metropolitan areas list Alcoholics Anonymous and other groups. If you live in a region without a social service network, you will probably need to travel some distance to find an appropriate group, but getting away for a twelve-step meeting should prove to be a blessing because anonymity is not easily found in rural precincts.

One more thing is exceedingly important for addicted pastors. Seek spiritual guidance within your religious tradition. Being in recovery from addiction is achievable for anyone, but it is always a lifelong project, so nurture and encouragement from your faith community are crucial elements in keeping the recovery going day by day, year by year. Humility helps, too.

CHAPTER 9

Denial

Denial is an incredibly strong force. It is perhaps the single most well-developed psychological force that clergy use. Pastors are well disposed to be in denial, if for no other reason than because of seminary and denominational training. Denial is a profound problem confronting religious institutions today, and the institutions are at least partly responsible.

Denial is the phenomenon of the human brain through which people refuse to see or acknowledge selected parts of reality. They may shut off remembrance and recognition of certain behaviors, events, or other realities, or more subtly, they may rationalize them away. In the context of this chapter, denial can be conscious or unconscious and includes repression, wherein a thought, idea, or experience is submerged into the unconscious. Repression is often associated with traumatic or painful events from the past, so any current situation that reminds one of the painful past may be denied through repression.

People in denial may seem to be untruthful about not recognizing a particular situation, but usually, they really do not see it, at least consciously. If they are lying, they are lying to themselves. In some circumstances, people in apparent denial may know what is going on but refuse to acknowledge it before others. This misrepresentation of reality is not so much denial as it is dishonesty.

Repeatedly, I have sat in my office listening to pastors pour out stories of strange and irresponsible behavior, usually their own, but they have no sense at all that anything is amiss. I am not referring here only to major misbehavior such as sexual seduction of parishioners. Pastors seem to be adept at denying ordinary, day-to-day actions and events. The bumptious common life of the parish they erase from consciousness, and the needs of their families and parishioners (and even their own needs) they fail to see. The manifest manipulations of the day, large and small, go unrecognized. It can be anything that does not fit into the neat mental frameworks they have constructed about themselves, other people, and God. Examples of pastoral denial come from every chapter in this book.

People who are attracted to careers in ministry tend to be intellectually bright and possess active imaginations. Certainly, imagination and intelligence are gifts that are needed as pastors seek to communicate with parishioners effectively and with freshness week after week. But the combination of these two gifts can be dangerous as well.

When the stresses and unromantic realities of pastoral life become difficult to bear, it is tempting for a pastor to create and live in a make-believe world. The more creative, bright, and imaginative the pastor, the easier it is to create a fantasy parish to replace the troubling real one. Denial is a major tool in such a creation. To live with a fantasy congregation, the pastor needs to block out the behaviors and demands of the actual parishioners. I suspect that virtually all pastors live in make-believe worlds to some extent, but the greater the time spent with fantasy congregations, the greater the danger that the pastor is in trouble from denial.

Institutions and Belief

As noted above, religious institutions and seminaries play roles in the problem of clergy denial. Depending on the denomination, seminaries can be instruments for reinforcing doctrines and traditions in the minds of seminarians, or they can be instruments for equipping future pastors to analyze and question their beliefs. Frequently, both functions are present in the same seminary curriculum, and both play a role in the problem of denial.

First, seminarians and pastors are surrounded by the requirement that they believe the doctrines and traditional teachings of the institutions they would serve. They need to believe certain things to maintain their own integrity and to meet the demands of the denomination. At least in the beginning, this is rarely a major problem. Thus, they acquiesce gladly in training that teaches them to look at the world through certain lenses. Sometimes these lenses are distorted, and sometimes these lenses refract out the fine grit of parish life so that pastors do not see—are not able to see—what is really going on. All events are to be understood and interpreted through the prism of the denomination's belief system, and things that do not fit are ignored, devalued, condemned, or denied.

I hesitate to provide specific examples of this phenomenon lest I be accused of mocking some well-loved doctrine of a particular denomination. It is not my intent to pass judgment on the efficacy of any creed. The point is that all institutions have internal needs that do not necessarily track perfectly with the realities of the world around them, and these needs affect the behavior of the leaders within the organizations more than they affect the members. Pastors are motivated to believe the tenets of their denominations, or at least pretend they do, because their places within the structure of their organizations, acceptance among colleagues, and often their economic livelihoods depend on it. The path of least resistance, therefore, is to deny the validity of any intellectual developments, social movements, or other claims that would threaten their comfortable place within the Church.

Pastors have many other reasons for believing the teachings of their denominations. They believe because they recognize them to be logical and true, because they have been taught them from childhood, because they have been persuaded by other people, or because they have experienced dramatic conversions in the contexts of their traditions. Most certainly they believe because they want to believe. The problem is not why they believe certain things but what they deny as a result of it.

Of course, seminarians and pastors accept the doctrines and traditions of their denominations in varying degrees. Different religious institutions have wider or narrower tolerance for dissent among their clergy, and some belief systems are broader and more inclusive than others. Nevertheless, both explicit education and tacit expectations from the institution are strong motivators that dispose some pastors toward denial in the conduct of their ministries.

Hermeneutics and Rationalization

The other factor people frequently learn in seminary is both congruent with and contrary to the first. Religious institutions make claims that if taken to extremes would be absurd. Passages can be found in scripture that contradict other passages, and some biblical accounts seem fanciful if taken literally. Therefore, seminarians are taught how to interpret the doctrines and scriptures of their denominations so that they make sense within the context of their traditions. Through training in hermeneutics, ironically, they are trained also in methods of rationalization. They are trained how to explain away the hard questions and develop whatever meaning the institution requires from any given text. This is congruent with the needs of the institution, but it can lead to results the institution does not intend. That is, the ends to which this skill can be taken may not be justified by what the institution means. Because of this training, a well-educated pastor has available the mental tools to make any creed or biblical text mean what the pastor wants it to mean in the context the pastor constructs, regardless of the denomination's traditional understanding. Herein lie the seeds of contrariness, for in the unsupervised arena of parish ministry, the temptation to undisciplined hermeneutical practice is great.

A relatively harmless form is a pastor doing slipshod exegetical work or taking lazy shortcuts with a text. However, the danger of doctrinal malpractice arising from the unrestrained use of this interpretive training is real. Pastors can lead their flocks into doctrinal box canyons where they can be spiritually or physically abused. David Koresh is an extreme example of this phenomenon, leading his Branch Davidian followers to their deaths with his bizarre use of the Book of Revelation. Mainline pastors would be more subtle, but I have counseled with parishioners who trusted their pastors' idiosyncratic teachings to the point where they suffered extreme guilt or other psychological ills. The aberrant behavior characteristic of cult leaders can be found in various lesser intensities in any denomination.[1]

A more common problem is that pastors are lured into applying their interpretation and rationalization skills to the conduct of their own lives. If they can convince their congregations that certain passages mean certain things, regardless of the plain meaning of the sentences, they can convince themselves of the goodness of their own actions, regardless of the harmful effect the actions may have on others or themselves. Thus, they can rather easily deny any problem.

To make matters worse, many congregations tend to give wide latitude to the pastor. Members hesitate to challenge the religious authority figure among them. Respect for the office prevents some people from complaining until the pastor's behavior becomes openly outrageous. Even then a few folks would rather be quiet and pray for miraculous improvement than address the problem behavior. And codependent board members protect their pastor from the wrath of any who would complain. Usually, too, the pastor is the last to hear of any unhappiness or complaints. All these elements give the pastor's denial mechanism time to become fully operational and secure. The more deeply into denial a pastor is, the more difficult it is to get the pastor out of it. All this denial and delayed response to it then sets the stage for a tragic drama.

In other chapters I have noted the narrow range of congregational tolerance within which most pastors work. Denial systems represent a temporary exception. When a pastor and key leaders in a parish, such as the matriarch, patriarch, or dominant board members, work together to hold back criticism of the pastor, this limited range of tolerance will become distorted. Another way of saying this is the public accountability of the pastor to the congregation will be thwarted. Some congregations, then, become codependent in support of the public persona of their dysfunctional pastor. The classic example is a charismatic narcissistic pastor with a dependent or compliant congregation. This pastor will recruit staff and board members who can be counted on to protect the pastor from critics. This human buffer zone can provide protection, sometimes for years, but eventually, a few credible complaints about the pastor's behavior will creep out around the edges. Once the protective wall has been breached, increasing numbers of angry parishioners will besiege the pastor in denial.

Confrontation or Crisis

So, what can be done to change this unfolding tragedy? Congregations that support telling the truth as normative can exert much influence over pastors who drift into denial. A healthy accountability prevails in such congregations, which prevents egregious damage from clerical denial. But the truth is often subjective in parish life, and congregations or boards caught up in codependent support of their pastors find it exceedingly difficult to challenge the alternate reality of their pastors until the problems escalate to crisis, at which time governing bodies typically intervene. Counseling or psychotherapy is an appropriate response, but getting a pastor who is in denial to seek this help usually requires confrontation or crisis.

Crisis is the more effective means because it represents the climax of a series of events that have come crashing together at a particular time and place. A crisis demands attention. No one easily gives up the mechanism of denial, and pastors working their ways through crises often continue to rationalize and deny the more painful aspects of their difficulties, but at least their attentions are focused on the problems. That is, they find explanations for their situations that are easier to accept than the bald reality. As a temporary step toward a growing acceptance of the truth, this is not necessarily bad. Pastors in crisis who merely replace one form of denial with another and remain stuck there, however, represent a significant challenge to those who would try to help.

The downside of a crisis is that people around the problem pastor who have some power or responsibility have to sit back and let the crisis happen. They need the patience and courage to allow events to take their natural courses into the pain-filled depths.

Confrontation is more effective when the problem behavior and denial are relatively minor. The sooner into a problem the confrontation occurs, the better the chances for some good to come of it. But most people are not sure enough of themselves or observant enough of the situation to enter into a confrontation with a pastor until it is too late. Alas, this is true for pastoral colleagues as well as parishioners. When confrontations do occur in situations where the problems and level of denial are great, they are not likely to be effective unless carefully planned by a group of people who know well the circumstances and personalities involved.

A small number of pastors suffer from serious personality disorders, narcissistic personality disorder being a common example. Such pastors repeatedly use and abuse people to meet their own needs, and of course, denial is a major tool in their arsenals of predatory behavior. These pastors rarely respond favorably to therapeutic intervention, and in any case they do not belong in ministry. Many other pastors struggle with personality problems that hurt parishioners and family members, but they are not sociopathic. From crises and confrontations these pastors can come to acknowledge their behaviors and grow from the experience. Those who remain in denial will continue to abuse people, even if unwittingly, leading them toward failed ministries. Those who accept the reality of their woundedness and seek appropriate healing can salvage their ministries and even bring exceptional blessings to the congregations they serve.

A Note about Conflict Avoidance

Many pastors confess with a hint of pride that they are conflict avoiders, conflict management training notwithstanding. It is not at all unusual for a pastor to hide from a problem parishioner or to pretend publicly that an unpleasant situation does not exist. Consciously avoiding an unpleasant encounter is not denial, and it is not necessarily bad. Pastors naturally use a variety of conflict management styles in different situations, and avoidance sometimes is the best style.2 In many cases avoidance may be practicing well the art of diplomacy. It is often an excellent tactic in short-term conflict situations. Let some time pass. Let emotions calm. Let passions cool.

Pastors may intentionally withdraw from parishioners for brief periods of time to avoid creating or exacerbating conflict, but tact must be exercised and the interval must be short. Over extended periods, however, pastors must reengage with their congregations, regardless of how painful, embarrassing, or unpleasant that may be. Parishioners who disagree with their pastors may be able to withdraw from the relationship with pastor or congregation with impunity, but pastors cannot do the same. An angry parishioner may avoid personal contact with or even shun a pastor, but the pastor may not reciprocate, except briefly as noted above. Members expect pastors to initiate attempts at reconciliation, even if ultimately, reconciliation fails. This is another tacit expectation associated with paying dues.

Pastors who continuously avoid involvement with parishioners who disagree with them or who challenge them in some way are at risk of producing conflict or raising the level of conflict in their congregations. Conflict avoidance is a tactic, not a strategy. It may bring a truce but not peace. It should be used sparingly.

Invisible and Invincible

As a military intelligence officer in Viet Nam, I experienced a peculiar phenomenon that I observed also in other soldiers. I had charge of an interrogation team that followed the infantry on their operations. Often we traveled with combat units as they moved through jungle and rubber plantations into rice paddies and villages. I remember riding outside and on top of armored personnel carriers, crashing through jungle toward some operational objective. Other times we traveled unaccompanied by Jeep through rural roads that were periodically mined by Viet Cong guerrillas. Clearly, we were in jeopardy of being shot at or blown up. And yet most of the time I was surrounded by a delusion that I was safe in the midst of danger. My young mind told me I was invincible and providentially protected from harm. Anyone else might be a target for enemy fire but not me. I could not believe that it could happen to me.

As it happened, I was lucky. The only wounds I received in Viet Nam were psychic ones, the kind that do not count for Purple Hearts. But since then, as I have observed ecclesiastical guerrilla warfare and congregational combat, I have seen pastors exhibiting the same kind of denial that I did in Viet Nam. Compared with military combat, the risks are different in church wars. I am tempted to say that violent death is not a factor in ecclesiastical conflict, but historically, this is not true. Many people of faith have suffered torture and death at the hands of church authorities and religious zealots.

We no longer burn people at the stake for heresy, yet in the context of current North American congregational life there remain serious risks associated with denial. The first risk is that faithful ministry will not be carried out. Good news will not be proclaimed authentically, and the spiritual and sometimes physical health of parishioners will be put in jeopardy. The spiritual vitality and physical well-being of pastors are at risk here, as well as their calls to ministry. Nevertheless, many pastors in the midst of conflict continue to deny that there are any problems. Others operate in ways guaranteed to produce congregational trauma and delude themselves that nothing is wrong.

The unsupervised nature of pastoral ministry acts as an emotional incubator, surrounding pastors with warmth and a sense of protection that allows them to wander from responsible conduct without challenge. For some, the experience of crossing conventional boundaries without being challenged or confronted is too alluring to resist. This is true whether the boundaries crossed are doctrinal or ethical, in word or deed, and relate to congregational leadership or personal life. After frolicking across the border for a time without being ordered back, pastors may develop a delusional sense of invisibility or invincibility, accompanied by a strong sense of being held in grace. These feelings are particularly associated with pastors who transgress sexual boundaries. It is easy then for pastors to deny that their behavior is harmful since no one is complaining, including God. The irony is that they may indeed be held in grace by God, quite apart from whether God approves, but if they continue to wander too far from responsible pastoral behavior, for too long a time, they will eventually come to crisis. In that case, it is not likely that their congregations or their denominations will hold them in the same grace that God does.

Congregations can help pastors maintain appropriate boundaries by insisting on some system of accountability. A strong personnel committee, not handpicked by the pastor, that meets with the pastor regularly (quarterly or at least semiannually) is one way. Meetings between the pastor and the personnel committee could be scheduled to affirm effective pastoral performance and identify areas of concern. These meetings should be separate from the process of compensation review. Governing bodies could assign mentors to pastors and arrange for the mentors to have access to congregational feedback. Boards can reasonably ask for reports on pastoral activities (home visitation, hospital calls, etc.) as long as pastoral confidentiality is respected.

Pastors whose behavior and demeanor have been troubling to their congregations long enough for complaints to circulate publicly often continue to deny any problems. A typical response from such a pastor is, "Even if appearances are questionable, I haven't done anything wrong." In some cases it may be, upon investigation, that the pastor has not technically committed any ecclesiastical offense, but to a congregation upset by the observed behavior of the pastor, perception is reality. In parish ministry, the appearance of impropriety *is* impropriety. This is a refinement of the adage "where there's smoke there's fire." The smoke is the fire. The very presence of circumstances that are embarrassing and may be improper is a problem for a congregation, and the profoundest pastoral denial will not erase the subject from the minds of parishioners once they acknowledge their observations. And in cases where there really is fire, no amount of denial will save the pastor from self-destruction.

Denial and rationalization can't save your ministry if you are acting irresponsibly. In parish settings, they are like embers waiting for any breeze to provoke them into flame. And the worst suffering comes not from the inevitable ecclesiastical fires but from the psychic scars that remain long after the fury has run its course.

Vigilant self-awareness can save you. Be unflinchingly honest with yourself about everything you do in ministry. Examine your motives regularly. Recognize your evil impulses, but don't fear them. They will hurt you more if you deny having them than if you bring them into consciousness where you can keep track of them. Confess your sins to yourself and God. Acknowledge, also, the good work you produce, but don't be seduced into thinking that your good work entitles you to take advantage of others.

And to ensure the success of your antidenial efforts, find a friend to confide in who cares enough about you to give you honest feedback about how you are doing. Blessed are you whose friends tell you the truth about yourself.

CHAPTER 10

Conditional Love

Never have I met a pastor who did not relish being well loved by members of the congregation. All too often, however, I have encountered pastors who did not relish loving their parishioners. This, in my estimation, is the number one factor that creates trouble for pastors. Far and away the single greatest complaint I have heard from parishioners, though phrased in a variety of ways, can be expressed in one short sentence: "Our pastor doesn't love us."

Every once in a while a disgruntled member will add, "And that's what pastors get paid for." Well, there are words for people who get paid for their love, but *pastor* isn't one of them. Regardless of the widespread misapprehension that pastors are professionals (in the sense of getting paid rather than in the sense of professing a life's work), congregations can't and don't pay pastors to love them. Genuine pastoral affection has never depended on remuneration. This kind of love is a gift mediated through pastors (and others) by the grace of God. It may be sought in prayer and earnestly cultivated. Nevertheless, authentic pastoral love is all tangled up with human brokenness and sin; thus, in various ways its expression may be impaired.

Hobbling Hearts

People who are inherently misanthropic are rarely drawn to ministry. Virtually all pastors believe themselves to be loving, caring, compassionate people. The sociopath who is drawn to ministry for the gratification of personal needs and who preys on the vulnerabilities of parishioners for self-satisfaction is an exception who needs to be considered separately. Sociopaths would claim to love parishioners, but they do so in harmful and excessive ways solely to scratch their own twisted itches. This work is not about the occasional sociopath who slips into parish ministry. Such a person would ignore it anyway. Yet this factor of conditional love is commonly found among the broad range of otherwise competent pastors.

The problem is not that pastors do not love but that they love in ways that are not fully integrated and healthy. Love, in such halfhearted circumstances, does not contribute to the well-being of parishioners. What follows are some of the ways that pastors hobble their hearts and thus their ministries.

Some pastors live for the Church. They are swept up in affection for institutions and traditions, and they loyally and proudly carry the banners of their denominations. They are more deeply concerned about events and developments in the distant Church than in their congregations. They love the Church more than they love the people (who really are the church), and the problem is that the people perceive this. Congregants are given regular messages that the intangible, abstract, disembodied, and mysterious institutional entity that is called the Church is a jealous lover, demanding all from their pastors, and their pastors happily oblige. By loving the Church more than the people, these pastors communicate that the light of God as reflected through the structure of their denominations is better, purer, and more worthy of love than the light of God as reflected through the lives of the real people they have been called to serve.

Of course, pastors must love the Church and be loyal to the institutions they serve. But if pastors give energy, enthusiasm, and attention disproportionately to the ethereal idea of the Church rather than to the incarnate lives of the souls in their parishes, trouble will inevitably arise.

A different form of this failure of affection involves pastors' expectations from parishioners. This is love contingent on behavior. That is, some pastors will pour out affection according to how parishioners respond to their messages or obey their explicit or implicit demands. Since members are likely to respond in widely varying ways, the door is opened to perceptions that the pastor plays favorites among parishioners.

It is only natural that a pastor would like some people more than others. Any effective pastor should be sensitive to this problem to avoid the trap of being seen to play favorites. But love contingent on behavior is a more insidious problem. It is not simply liking some people more than others because they agree with the pastor or have more in common with the pastor. It is the active withholding of care and affection from certain people because they have not changed, accepted the message, or obeyed the wishes of the pastor. A pastor can do this very subtly and with many nuances. Frequently, a pastor is not even conscious of the expression of this contingent love. However, parishioners pick it up, in varying degrees of awareness, and it breeds resentment among them.

By far the most common expression of conditional love is the pastor's refusal or inability to accept people as they are and where they are. This lack of acceptance goes back to the matter of unrealistic expectations. People in parishes are not necessarily perfect pilgrims with fully developed understandings of the teachings of the faith. They can be well insulated from the precious wisdom of the Church, rough-edged, self-indulgent, deficient in ethical sensitivity, misguided, and emotionally unstable. They can also be well educated, articulate, devout, faithful, sane, and hale. If any characteristic is common to all parishioners, it is that they have been touched by the pandemic of human pain and caught up in the web of human sin and are yet held in grace by God. Whatever their lot, however, they are who they are, and a pastor's disappointment that they are not otherwise will not change this reality.

Pastors create interesting ironies when they preach love and care for poor, sick, and outcast people of the world while rejecting people in their congregations who may be poor in spirit, sick in soul, or ignorant of respectability.

One form of this nonacceptance of parishioners is passive avoidance of them. Pastors are more likely to stay away from people they do not like than they are to express actively their negative feelings about them On a temporary basis, avoidance of a particular person may be a good strategy if unproductive conflict would result from a face-to-face meeting. But a pastor cannot avoid relating to an entire congregation without sending a strong signal that the pastor does not love them.

That signal is sent by the pastor's absence from places and occasions where and when members of the congregation would like to see the pastor present. In small towns, for example, not being seen downtown, not strolling the sidewalk along Main Street, and not greeting folks in the square may be perceived as signals of conditional love. In other settings, not supporting the local high school football team may be a signal. If a pastor never visits the kindergarten church school class or never stops by the senior high fellowship meetings, such absences will be noted and taken as evidence that the groups are not valued.

Loving Them Anyway

No human is completely capable of loving other humans unconditionally. Only God loves fully without condition. But pastors, more than others, are responsible for trying harder to emulate the eternal presence of God's love. By the nature of the calling to ministry, pastors represent symbolically the interests of God, and they must therefore work hard to meet people where the people are and not where the pastors are. It is not necessary to agree with someone's ignorant ideas or condone a person's unhealthy lifestyle to accept that person as a human being created in the image of God and loved by God. It is not even necessary to like someone to express love.

A challenge in this regard is for pastors to care for parishioners who exhibit active dislike for them. Female pastors, for example, sometimes encounter parishioners who object to women in the pulpit. A few of these folks respond with open belligerence, while others adopt passive-aggressive tactics. By and large, female pastors have responded to these detractors by ignoring the rancor and loving them anyway—which is the smart thing to do.

A few years ago an interesting event unfolded with a female pastor who was called to a rural parish where no woman had ever served before. Several die-hard members made it clear they did not like having a woman preach to them, but she wisely chose not to take it as personal rejection, and she reached out to them with affection despite their resistance. Several weeks after she began work, an incident occurred that turned the situation around. A local pastor from a denomination that did not allow the ordination of women publicly snubbed her on the street in the village.

When news of the incident spread rapidly throughout the parish, her entire congregation, including her detractors, rallied around her; thereafter, they proudly embraced her as their pastor. Because one of their own had been treated rudely in public by an outsider from another church, the people needed to respond in a way that transcended old social traditions about the pulpit being for men only. This story might have had a different ending, however, if she had withheld pastoral attention from those who were unhappy with the imposition of a female pastor.

Pastors get into trouble when they withhold or express affection to parishioners according to how closely or distantly the parishioners agree with the pastors' positions. When pastors shun parishioners, flagrantly or subtly, because they are not sufficiently enlightened, the failure of light is not in the deficient members but in the hearts of the pastors.

Low Self-Esteem

Yet another conditional love phenomenon is somewhat the reverse of the above. My observation is that as a group, clergy are susceptible to low self-esteem, and low self-esteem creates barriers to expressing love for others in healthy ways. To expand on the biblical text, you can't love your neighbor as yourself if you don't love yourself. Some pastors fail to see anything lovable in their parishioners because they cannot see anything lovable in themselves. So, if there is any motivation for a pastor to be a caring, accepting presence among the members of a congregation when there is no self-care or self-love, it may be for unhealthy reasons. Certainly codependent behavior, as discussed in chapter 7, is a possibility. Pastors with low self-esteem may reach out with affection to parishioners in order to bolster a sense of inadequacy, to assuage a sense of unworthiness, or to seek someone to reciprocate those feelings. Pastors may also retreat quickly into indifference or hostility if their personal needs are not met this way.

Outward appearance is no indicator of self-esteem. Pastors with inadequate self-esteem may appear outwardly calm and confident but be riddled inwardly with doubt and insecurity. Ironically, the most intelligent and creative pastors seem the most prone to self-esteem problems. The greater the gifts, the greater the doubts, and the greater the abilities for high achievement, the greater the potential for getting into trouble. No matter how gifted, pastors who do not trust their own unconditional acceptance by God or believe their own worth in the eyes of God have trouble communicating love and grace to their parishioners.

When pastors place conditions on loving themselves, they tend also to love their parishioners in the same limited manner. Even healthy pastors have difficulty removing, as they become aware of them, the barriers they have consciously or otherwise set against accepting and caring for people in their congregations. So it is doubly difficult for pastors who are not emotionally whole.

A Note about Introversion and Extroversion

The North American population as a whole seems to be decidedly extroverted. Some groups within the larger population, such as Native Americans and Scandinavian Americans, may be more introverted, but extroversion is taken to be the norm, and introversion is sometimes presented as if something was deficient about it. This negative portrayal of introversion has strong implications for ministry because approximately half of the pastors I know are introverts, and since my pool of clergy acquaintances is many hundreds large, I suspect that this group is statistically representative. If we add to this number clergy who claim to be extroverts but act like introverts, there is a clear majority on the introvert side. Perhaps some of these conflicted extroverts claim to be such because they believe they must be people oriented to be successful pastors and they equate introversion with avoidance of people.

If many pastors are introverts and at least some parishioners regard introversion as an inadequacy in pastors, then problems may arise for introverted pastors. But extroverted pastors also have difficulties associated with their personalities. Both types face potential problems in ministry, and each has particular strengths that can aid in ministry. Introverts, for example, may find it easier than extroverts to communicate spiritual authenticity to their congregations. Extroverts may be more comfortable moderating large meetings. Both personality traits are valuable and needed in a healthy society.

Pastors have used both introversion and extroversion as excuses for their failures to love, care for, and accept parishioners. One introvert excuse is that people expect from them more personal interaction than they are capable of giving. "I'm not a people person," one will say. "I love my congregation, but I am not a glad-hander or backslapper," another will say. A third response will be, "The time I spend in solitary prayer for the people of the church is much more important than the time I spend with them in person."

My response to the first excuse is that being an introvert has no relationship to being or not being a people person. Introverts and extroverts are equally capable of being loving, caring presences among their parishioners. Introverts may be more comfortable in one-on-one and small group settings, and extroverts may be more comfortable in large groups, but both can be very effective pastors. A pastor who has difficulty relating to people, or who does not like being around people, has no business in parish ministry and needs to find another calling.

Concerning the second excuse, there is no reason why an introverted pastor should be a glad-hander or backslapper if this behavior is not comfortable or natural. Many congregations appreciate a degree of kindly reticence from the pastor. It is not necessary to be the life of the party to demonstrate affection for people. Indeed, a quiet sigh at a poignant moment may communicate more love than a hundred hugs or a thousand handshakes.

As to time in prayer being more important than time with the people, I would say that a pastor spending time with people *is* a pastor spending time at prayer. Certainly, private time for meditation and prayer is vital to the maintenance of spiritual health, especially for an introvert. But it is in no way superior to being among the people. The same applies to the claims for study time. While necessary, such time must be balanced with the equally important need for a public pastoral presence in the parish.

Extroverts do not need to work as hard at being out among the people, although extroverts are not immune to disliking people. While introverts in ministry run the risk of being perceived as indifferent or snobbish, extroverts are sometimes seen as superficial or insincere. They also tend to spend time explaining what they really meant to say because they previously said ill-considered things. They discover what they think by saying it out loud before reflecting on it. A major problem for an extroverted pastor is saying too much.

In pastoral visitation, for example, extroverts need to be aware of how much they talk. Some strongly extroverted pastors dominate their pastoral calls with unending streams of stories, observations, and chit-chat, allowing their parishioners little or no chance to speak. This tendency can be entertaining at times, but pastors who are good talkers need to be sensitive to the needs of parishioners to tell *their* stories, reveal *their* concerns, and pour out *their* confessions. Extroverted pastors must devote particular attention to listening because listening to the parishioner is the primary task of pastoral visitation.

One extroverted pastor I know has carefully developed a list of questions to draw out conversation from people. Unthinkingly, however, this pastor often moves impatiently to the next question if the parishioner's response is thoughtfully slow. Also, this pastor is tempted to jump in with a personal story a parishioner's answer brings to mind. The valuable effort this pastor puts into asking just the right questions can be completely undone by these ill-considered, untimely interventions.

In one-on-one settings or in small groups some introverts talk too much. A number of introverted pastors who will speak little in large gatherings feel quite comfortable doing the talking when making pastoral visits, and they may dominate these conversations without being aware of it. Pastors know that when visiting homebound folks, they will encounter some who will latch on to them with streams of talk, which makes it difficult to leave gracefully. But some pastors do a similar thing by talking so much they miss their parishioners' signals that it is time to say farewell.

Generally, however, introverted pastors are at risk of listening too much. One parishioner told me of a visit by her new (and, as it turned out, strongly introverted) pastor shortly after her husband had died. The pastor sat in a chair opposite her and said nothing for a long time. The pastor felt that his presence alone was enough; simply being in the room with the grieving woman was sufficient to demonstrate care. So he continued to sit across from her without speaking. After some minutes the woman could stand the silence no longer and began to lead the conversation, which succeeded in evoking only short responses from her pastor. Subsequent visits from the pastor over the next several months produced the same pattern of noncommunication, which upset the woman a great deal.

In some settings, being present in silence is indeed beneficial. When a parishioner is near death from cancer, the quiet presence of the pastor sitting beside the hospital bed, perhaps holding the patient's hand, is sufficient. When sitting through the night with a parishioner in the waiting room of the coronary care unit, awaiting news of surgery, long periods of silence are normal. But in most situations, introverts need to pay attention to being adequately conversational, just as extroverts need to monitor how much they speak.

When complaints arise about lack of pastoral affection, an extroverted pastor may protest, "What do you mean I don't love them? I've made a hundred pastoral calls this month." Another may say, "I've joined every service club in this town and go to meetings every night of the week. What more do they want?" Yet another may claim, "All these denominational committees I serve on are more important than the do-nothing little committees in my parish."

In response to the first excuse, I would say that seventy times seven pastoral calls would not demonstrate love if the visits were perfunctory or superficial or made for the purpose of counting them for a report. There is a significant difference between being in the presence of another person and being present with another person. Being present requires active attention to the words and affect of the other person. An ineffable quality of pastoral caring is communicated when the love is authentically present, but if it is not, sooner or later people will perceive the missing affection. Even the most charming extrovert, if love is absent, will be exposed as a phony in due time.

To the second, I would say that joining clubs and attending meetings, while worthy things to do, are not demonstrations of affection for the people of the congregation. This may be a way of supporting certain members of the congregation who also belong to the organizations, but if carried too far, it robs time from a greater number of parishioners. Pastors who participate in many extraparish activities may be satisfying their own needs and not those of the parish. This is not necessarily bad for an extremely extroverted pastor as long as the pastor does not rationalize the activities as ministry for the congregation. In any case, the call to ministry is not a call to frenetic extracurricular socializing.

As far as denominational meetings are concerned, again, the question of balance arises. Such meetings may be more interesting than parish meetings, but time spent with colleagues doing denominational business is not more important in the scheme of the universe than time spent with the choir picnic committee of the local parish. In the context of whether or not a pastor cares about the people in the congregation, the choir picnic committee is clearly more important.

You, whether introvert or extrovert, need to work hard at maintaining conversational balance with your parishioners. Too much chatter and too many accounts of things of personal interest to you can be harmful. Too little of these likewise can undermine an otherwise effective ministry.

An Experiment

A few years ago I tried an experiment with conversation among introverts and extroverts. I was teaching a class of about fifty church members and pastors at a denominational event. The people came from many
different churches and knew one another superficially, if at all. With that
many people in one room, a few extroverts can quickly dominate any
conversation, and the introverts will sit back and say nothing. So I divided the class into two discussion groups according to their own self-desig-
nations as introverts or extroverts. About one-third identified themselves
as introverts. I further divided them within these larger groups according
to whether they preferred listening or talking. About two-thirds of the
extroverted group preferred talking. The introverted group split about
evenly, so the result was two small groups of introverts and one medium-
sized and one large group of extroverts. All four groups were given the
same topic for discussion.

When we reconvened in plenary, each group was asked to report on
the conversational participation of its members. The two extroverted
groups, those who preferred listening and those who preferred speaking,
reported that everyone participated easily in the discussion. But they ran
out of time because so much talking occurred. The introverts who preferred talking also experienced full participation and expressed pleasure
at how easy it was for this to happen. The introverts who preferred
listening provided the surprise. They were astonished not just that all of
them spoke but that they all spoke at length, practically buzzing nonstop.
It was a new experience for them.

Pastors would do well to be sensitive not only to their own speaking
dynamics but also to those of their parishioners, especially in board and
committee meetings. Those who remain silent during discussions may
be introverts or possibly extroverts who are insecure about speaking out.
Effective pastors will find ways of providing safe time and opportunity
for the quiet ones to enter into the conversation. They will thereby facili-
tate many thoughtful comments that the group would otherwise be de-
prived of.

Unhobbling Hearts

Well, then, what can be done for pastors who love conditionally? Some answers have been suggested already in previous chapters: psychotherapy, spiritual direction, prayer. Nevertheless, pastors cannot be taught to love people. Sensitivity encounter groups have enjoyed a certain following over the past few decades as vehicles for helping people get in touch with their own feelings with, I suspect, mixed results. The pastors I have known who have gone through sensitivity training have gained a great deal of self-awareness, but they have not necessarily connected that with any feelings of affection for their congregations.

Pastors who would unhobble their hearts must find some internal motivation. They must release something inside so that the love of God already there can radiate out to other people. And other people can help, too, but there is no instruction manual. Ultimately, there is only the grace of God.

Here is some good news. People want to be known and loved by their pastor. They want to feel accepted and secure in a parish-pastor relationship. If they feel acceptance and love they will inevitably grant wide latitude for their pastor to work on hobbyhorses, arcane theological studies, or personal goals. This is a beneficial side effect that derives from healthy and authentic pastoral affection.

Coda

The coda to this song of pastoral love is this: Not only do you need to love your parishioners, but you need to let your parishioners love you. Church members want to show affection for their pastors and do so in a variety of ways, including giving small gifts. If you habitually shun this affection, for whatever reason, you send messages of rejection to your congregation. If you are wise, you will accept these demonstrations of love with good humor, thanks, humility, and grace.[1]

The Promised Land

The practice of religion can be associated with a number of opposing dual constructs: law and grace, transcendence and immanence, obedience and freedom, among others. For the practice of parish ministry one dualism that comes to mind is romance and realism. Many seminarians and young pastors are infatuated with ministry, inhaling the romantic aromas of leading worship, heroically saving lost souls, and humbly glorying in the adoration of grateful parishioners. Few pastors at retirement age retain much of their youthful romantic ideation. But some do: the fortunate ones.

Romanticism is not a bad thing. Being called to ministry is like falling in love; therefore, a time of honeymooning is needed for the prospective pastor to savor the developing relationship with a congregation. The romantic element in ministry acts as a lure to the imagination in ways the realistic element cannot. A romantic spirit can keep ministry fresh year after year when the prosaic realities would cause it to go stale.

But, of course, it is not enough. A well-balanced ministry requires a realistic outlook. Some problems may never be solved. Some troubled situations may need to be managed indefinitely rather than resolved. Some parishioners may never rise out of narrow-mindedness or mean-spiritedness. All pastors are imperfect human beings who make mistakes and bad decisions from time to time. The crucial factor that keeps romanticism from becoming denial and keeps realism from turning into cynicism is responsibility. Responsibility is a force, fueled by truth and love, which brings healthy power to both elements.

Parish ministry requires responsible service and responsible leadership, and service and leadership require both romantic and realistic qualities. To serve a congregation, a pastor needs to see the possibilities in people, a romantic quality, but also see the people as they are, a realistic one. To lead requires courage, a romantic quality, and practical knowledge, a realistic one.

The Ego Factor

Carl Jung called the total personality of an individual the Self. The Self includes ego, subconscious, shadow—all the mental functioning of a person. The goal of the Self is to integrate self-knowledge of all its various components, gifts, talents, desires, and so on into a healthy well-functioning personality. Transposing to the religious dimension, I would say that an integrated Self is more open to the will of God than a splintered Self. Concomitantly, ministry that is Self-directed is more effective than ministry dominated by only one aspect of personality.

The element of personality that is most likely to influence a pastor in unproductive ways is the ego. Ego plays a major role in the sense of being called to ministry. The public claim that God has chosen one to represent God before the people is loaded with ego dynamics. Ego-connected motivations for hearing a call to ministry may include the desire for respect or nurture or audience. Ego-driven ministry seeks upward mobility, moving only to larger or more important parishes. Ego-driven ministry values prestige over performance and style over authenticity. Ego-driven ministry is possessive. Pastors with overactive egos think of their congregations as personal possessions. Such pastors apply the word *my* without reflection to people or groups. "I'll have my board take care of your request for a wedding in my sanctuary," for example, or "My associate pastor will visit you when you go into the hospital." When ego dominates parish relationships, resentments will build. When ego dominates a pastor's decision-making process, the ministry is flawed.

By way of confession, here is a personal example. The position I hold is associate executive in a midlevel governing body in the Presbyterian Church (USA). From the affirmation I have received from colleagues, I would judge that I am effective in my work, and I believe that God has given me the gifts for the special kind of ministry I am doing. I am happier and more satisfied in my present position than in any other work I have done. However, being associate executive is not as prestigious or powerful as being executive presbyter, and sometimes my ego dreams of applying for an executive presbyter position. Romantically, I believe I could do a competent job as executive presbyter, but realistically, I know that I would not be happy or satisfied carrying out some of the responsibilities of that position. My ego wants me to move up, but my Self wants me to do what I do best without regard to prestige or power. For healthy wholeness, I need to allow my ego room to play, but my ego needs to cooperate with the rest of me, following the wiser discipline of my integrated Self.

Power and Responsibility

Temptations peculiar to pastoral ministry appear from time to time, and pastors need to recognize and name them. They arise out of the strengths that pastors bring to their callings, such as analytical abilities, knowledge of people, and spiritual power. As a result, pastors may manipulate parishioners or take advantage of them for personal gratification. An extreme example is a pastor engaging in sexual activities with a parishioner, but less egregious behaviors also arise from temptations associated with these pastoral strengths. Some pastors find it hard to manage the power they acquire from the exercise of ministry. Trusting their pastors, certain parishioners will reveal their vulnerabilities to them, opening themselves to healing or harm, depending on how the pastors respond.

Spiritual power, of course, can be used for good or evil. Spiritually mature pastors acknowledge this and accept that they are capable of evil as well as good. All pastors will encounter temptations to use or abuse their parishioners, but the responsible ones will recognize them and confess their shadowed urges in ways appropriate to their traditions.

Responsibility is the key to effective ministry. The pastor who behaves responsibly, leads responsibly, listens responsibly, and is responsible about self-care will thrive. The norms defining responsibility will vary from denomination to denomination, generation to generation, and cultural setting to cultural setting, but the ten major topics in this book form a framework for responsibility in the conduct of parish ministry. Seasoned pastors and newly ordained pastors can benefit from consideration of these subjects.

New pastors, in particular, need not suffer years of abuse from parishioners, from family members, and from themselves. Time invested early in ministry in avoiding or overcoming any of these perils will be well spent in building a foundation for a long and satisfying ministry.

Dreams of Ordination — and Nightmares

Some people would do better to spend time dealing with the problems raised in this book that affect them before taking on the demands of parish ministry. Realistically speaking, however, few seminarians approaching the day of ordination that they have dreamed about for years would appreciate the wisdom of delaying the acceptance of a call to parish ministry to work on personal issues. Not many would volunteer to postpone ordination once they have met all their denominational requirements. To do so would seem to cause great emotional pain to them. Nevertheless, in some cases making this hard decision would prevent even greater pain for prospective pastors and for members of congregations.

My observation is that ecclesiastical bodies charged with responsibility for oversight of candidates for ministry have difficulty saying "not yet" to those who need more time to prepare for ministry and "no" to those who are not suited for the demands of the calling. More often than not the hard decisions are simply not made, and marginal or psychologically unprepared people are funneled into the ranks of parish clergy.

Many people now seeking to be pastors have grown up in troubled households, have been addicts or codependents, have failed in marriages or careers, or have significant personality defects. Those who are under forty have suffered the ill effects of public education experiments in the United States that have resulted in lower standards and lower levels of academic competence among students compared to previous generations. Thus, pastors and seminarians who are in their forties or older are, in general, more skilled in reading, writing, and other communication skills relevant to ministry than pastors and seminarians who are younger.[1]

I had occasion to see this firsthand as a seminary student in the late 1970s. In a Church history class the professor assigned a three-page paper to the forty or so students. Each student was to write on a different topic to be selected from a list the professor provided. A second requirement was that each student place the paper on reserve in the library so that every student could read all the other students' papers. Reading those papers was an eye-opening experience for me.

With few exceptions, apart from varying levels of profundity, the papers written by students who had finished high school before the mid-1960s were well crafted. The papers written by those who had completed high school after the mid-1960s were replete with grammatical errors and misspellings. Some were disorganized and nearly unintelligible.

I had naively assumed that anyone who had been accepted into graduate school could write complete sentences and well-structured paragraphs. Not so. Conversations with seminary faculty members and my own experience as an adjunct professor have confirmed that this phenomenon is widespread.

Apart from this educational deficiency, however, I believe that the prevalence of dysfunction among seminarians and newly ordained pastors is no greater now than in past decades. This view is contrary to current conventional wisdom, but I base it on my work as a pastor to pastors among clergy of all ages.

Generations of Dysfunction

The problem behaviors that can be found among seminarians and new pastors today can be found commonly among clergy who have been serving congregations for ten, twenty, or forty years. Listening to stories about pastors who were active in the 1930s and 1940s leads me to conclude that this phenomenon has been with us for a long time. Ministry seems to attract troubled people who seek to resolve their own pain through tending to the pain of others, and this probably has been the situation for many generations. Ministry also attracts people who have experienced varying degrees of healing in the midst of a caring church community and who seek to return the favor by pursuing parish ministry.

Today religious institutions are held in lower esteem by the general public than in decades past. This perception can be attributed in part to the dysfunctional behavior of pastors who have been ill-serving their denominations for many years. The media spare no effort in publicizing the foibles and failures of prominent clergy—and rightly so. Pastors are public figures who are no less accountable to their parishioners than are public officials to the general public.

Yet there is cause for hope amidst all these signs of failure. There is a significant difference between the new generation of seminarians and pastors and those who have been serving for many years. This difference is good news. While the percentage of pastors with troubled lives has probably remained steady for generations, until recently, pressures from ecclesiastical institutions and the larger society have caused pastors to cover up or deny their problems. That is no longer the case. Changes in the larger society have made it much more acceptable, even fashionable, for people to acknowledge their dysfunctions and failures. And religious institutions have been the beneficiaries of this essentially secular phenomenon.

The hope-filled difference is that current seminarians and new pastors are much more apt to be honest about their woundedness than those who have gone before. They may have failed in careers and marriages, they may be recovering addicts, they may be pursuing parish ministry with uncertain motives, but they are less apt to be in denial. These people have been dissatisfied with other work, disappointed with other relationships, and traumatized by tragic events, yet have found something compelling and reassuring in the Church. These people have fallen into the depths of defeat and have experienced resurrection in the context of a religious community. These people have lost everything and have gained back better than they ever had because they experienced God's restoration through the Church. Many of these people are stronger at the broken places. Their wounds have been exposed to the air of public scrutiny, and they have survived, even thrived, as a result. They have tasted the grace of God.

I believe these pastors will have a profound effect on their denominations in the early decades of the twenty-first century as they reach the middle years of their ministries. As they come into their most productive periods, they will lead the Church into an era of renewal characterized by greater honesty and openness. And perhaps they will be better pastors because they are acquainted enough with pain never to belittle the pain of others.

There is further good news. Pastors who have been denying their problems and pathologies for years can now face them with hope for better lives and more effective ministries in the years remaining to them. They do not need to wait for a new generation to replace them. No matter how old they may be or how long they have been practicing ministry, they can rise from the ashes of their own self-destructive behavior and be better pastors as a result.

Career Counseling

Denominations routinely send candidates for ministry to counseling centers for psychological and professional evaluation. There is no reason, however, why this service should be restricted to candidates. Career counseling can be immensely beneficial as a recurring experience throughout ministry. Many career development centers have effective programs for helping pastors evaluate their work and gifts objectively. Pastors who feel stuck or dissatisfied or simply tired can gain much from career counseling, and pastors who are not experiencing difficulties but have been in the same place for ten years or more can also benefit. Some pastors think that postordination career counseling would be a blot on their record, but denominational officials do not see it that way. Bishops and executives look favorably on pastors who seek to improve or change their ministries through career development center evaluations. They see the pastors' efforts as signs of health rather than pathology.

A Trip Well Taken

Over the years I have told seminarians that if they have not had a crisis of faith while in seminary, they have not been paying attention. One of the most important experiences in pastoral education is tearing down a naive faith and rebuilding a mature faith in its place. Broadening the field, I would extend that concept into the pastorate. Pastors who have not experienced some kind of crisis in ministry can expect one sometime in the future if they are paying attention. This is not a dire prediction; rather, it is grounds for hope.

God calls out to all people, pastors included, through the crises in their lives. God makes use of these situations because transformation and growth are wrought out of crises. The promised land of productive ministry is open to all who answer God's call to serve in this way, but the journey through the wilderness never has been a luxurious ride on a smooth road. Only those who are willing to walk in the dust and ruts will be able to understand fully the joy and satisfaction of a trip well-taken. Despite the trials, all can be well. Let it be well with all who seek the promised land of parish ministry.

The alchemies of ministry require
Untested pastors pass through ice and fire,
For those refined in heat and formed in cold
Will find their service transformed into gold.[2]

Pastors with Problem Pasts and Secret Lives

This subject does not fit into any one chapter but has associations with many themes addressed in this book, especially addictions, codependence, and denial. Problem pasts and secret lives represent two interrelated groups of pastors with four subgroups associated with each. The behaviors and experiences that produce these groupings arise from the timeless temptations of humankind: sex, money, and war. Sexual promiscuity and adulterous affairs seem to be the most common. Drug abuse and other addictions are not rare. Misappropriating money or other property weighs guiltily on a few. Some pastors who are combat veterans remain haunted years later by images of their own brutality. Pregnancy before marriage and abortions are secrets a number of female pastors carry. Many pastors were subjected to physical, emotional, or sexual abuse as children, and although these are matters for which they bear no responsibility, such experiences cause deep shame and often remain zealously guarded secrets. Regardless of the specific nature of the problems or secrets, the poignant distinctions to be made here concern how pastors deal with them.

Problem Pasts

These are the four types of pastors with problem pasts:

1. *Augustinians.* Like their namesake Augustine of Hippo, Augustinian pastors made moral mistakes in their earlier years, made public confession at some point, often in connection with a conversion experience, and have since become earnest supporters of their religious traditions. Also like Augustine, they tend to be obsessed with their past sins

and continue to feel personal guilt, which they never quite let go of. Augustinians can benefit greatly from spiritual direction and psychotherapy.

2. *Prodigals.* Like the prodigal in the parable, prodigal sons and daughters were engaged in wickedness in their earlier lives and have since made public confession. They are different from Augustinians in that they have accepted God's grace and have taken up ministry without guilt or undue brooding about past mistakes. Prodigals make very good pastors.

3. *Secret Augustinians.* These pastors have the guilt feelings and self-reproach of the Augustinians, but since they have never made public confession of their failings (in the context of the denominational structure), they live in fear of being found out and thrown out of ministry. Therapy and spiritual direction are needed for these pastors, and finding trustworthy friends to hear their confessions may be helpful for secret Augustinians.

4. *Secret Prodigals.* These are like prodigals except they have not disclosed their pasts to denominational officials, and they live with the fear that their secrets will be uncovered someday, and then they will be in trouble with their denominations. Secret prodigals do not worry as much as secret Augustinians, but they want to avoid the embarrassment of public scrutiny. They, too, can benefit from confessing to a trusted friend.

To Tell or Not to Tell

The question that arises for secret Augustinians and secret prodigals is whether they should disclose these matters to denominational officials. My answer is an equivocal maybe. It depends on the denominational ethos and the gravity of the secrets. How has the denomination responded to similar situations in the past? Is the denomination going through a reactionary process? It also depends on how likely disclosure by someone else may be and whether the secret sins predate ordination. With some exceptions, what was done before ordination is less a problem than what has been done since.

Another factor is the extent of the fear of discovery and whether it hampers productive ministry. At the very least a pastor should take these secrets and fears to a therapist who knows something about the particular denomination.

However, if accusations, rumors, or information about one's secret past should ever come to denominational officials from some other source, the officials are almost always obliged to look into the matter, and my unequivocal advice to pastors in such situations is to tell the truth. Once information, even if inaccurate, is in the hands of bishops or executives, the wheels of institutional inquiry will grind inexorably forward, and it is better to be honest up front than be deemed a liar later. Ecclesiastical discipline may result from telling the truth, but except for extreme cases, it will be milder than if the truth is denied. And, of course, with freely given confession, there is always the chance that the official response will be forgiveness and grace.

My observation is that denominational officers are not inclined to look into pastors' pasts as long as things are going well. They do not want to know anything that will cause them extra work or heartache. Inquisitions do not start in governing bodies. They start with angry or frightened individuals. Institutional inertia and executives with too many other fires to put out restrain governing bodies from hounding out behavioral heretics. But if sufficient numbers of grassroots church members rise up in complaint, denominational leaders can be forced to react punitively, and sometimes pastors with troubled pasts are sacrificed for the sake of the institution. This rarely happens, however, unless the troubled past impinges in some way on present performance. Even then, the first reaction of a governing body will be to protect the status quo, and that means protecting the pastor.

At various points in this book I have advised discretion concerning how much of their personal lives and spiritual struggles pastors should reveal to their parishioners. Discretion certainly applies to the subjects considered here. Elsewhere, however, I have described the positive values of pastors not being in denial about their failures, and the inference could be drawn that it would be good to make everything public. It would not. Being free from denial does not mean a pastor should let it all hang out in front of the congregation. Although pastors can be relatively open with colleagues and denominational officials about their earlier lives, they must use discretion in how much they reveal to parishioners, even indirectly.

It may be beneficial for a congregation to know, for example, that their pastor was addicted to drugs as a teenager, but no good purpose is served by shocking the congregation with all the sordid details of drug-induced behavior. In counseling an addicted parishioner, some of this information may be appropriate, but not from the pulpit. Certainly, it is fitting for a pastor to disclose a previous marriage to the congregation, but the congregation is not well served by a pastor who publicly announces all the reasons for the divorce, especially since such matters are subjective and only one side of the story is being told. Too much public self-disclosure by the pastor about sensitive matters may raise the concern among parishioners that the pastor can't be trusted to keep their sensitive matters confidential.

A few months ago I attended a service at a church of another denomination. I did not know the pastor, but it quickly became evident that she was a recovering addizct of some sort. The liturgical language she used was laced with buzzwords from the "recovering community." Twelve-step jargon and God talk were interwoven from the call to worship to the benediction, and the pastor repeatedly drew attention to her own personal issues in the course of worship. Pastors would do well to monitor how often they personalize the language of worship to focus attention on themselves. Done judiciously, this can provide inspiration to a congregation of struggling people. But if a pattern of "Look at me!" or "Woe is me!" characterizes the service of worship, the pastor may be abusing the congregation.

Secret Lives

To this point, the focus has been on pastors with failures in their pasts. There are those, however, who are living problematic secret lives right now, and they can be grouped into four categories:

1. *Deniers.* The problems of pastors in denial were discussed in chapter 9. A subtype could be added here to include sociopaths and pastors with narcissistic personality disorder. These pastors experience no guilt, appropriate or otherwise, although they make great efforts to keep their secret behavior secret. Making recommendations for the benefit of these pastors is an exercise in futility, so I will say no more.

2. *Practicing Augustinians.* These pastors are obsessed with their sinfulness, hate themselves for what they do, but continue to do it, fearing each day that they will be found out. Practicing Augustinians need to reread the chapters in this book pertinent to their behaviors and seek appropriate help.

3. *Practicing Prodigals.* These pastors are still living the prodigal life, knowing they are wasting their lives and their careers. They are confident they will soon be able to turn their lives around, and they know that God will welcome them home with grace, but they have not been able to change just yet. Some practicing prodigals believe that their behavior may be unacceptable to their denominations but perfectly fine with God. They also fear being caught, and they, too, need to follow the advice given above to practicing Augustinians.

4. *Homosexual Pastors.* This is a special group. Some commentators would quickly place homosexual pastors into one of the other groups, but I do not. Extensive ecclesiastical debates over the last quarter century have failed to produce any ecumenical consensus about the nature of homosexuality within the economy of God's creation. A few denominations ordain openly homosexual men and women, but most do not. Therefore, the great majority of homosexual pastors (whether celibate or with partners) live with the continuous dread of discovery and subsequent removal from ordained office. Homosexual pastors need counseling and support as much as any other pastors. However, because of their vulnerability to ecclesiastical discipline arising from who they are as much as from what they do, additional care is important. For the most part, this care should be sought outside denominational channels.

Living with Vulnerability

Many pastors are vulnerable to lesser or greater extents because of the circumstances of their lives, past and present. They face as little as embarrassment or as much as disgrace and removal from office. Some are subject to criminal prosecution in secular courts for sexually abusing children, for example, but these egregious cases do not fall within the scope of this appendix. The majority of pastors with problem pasts or secret present lives can salvage ministry if their secrets become public.

With regard to past problem behavior, those who can show that they have done therapeutic work on the problems usually can expect support from their denominations. If current secret behavior comes to light, again, most pastors can expect assistance from their denominations upon their agreement to get counseling and cooperate with official guidance. Defiant stances and massive denial in the face of credible evidence, however, will not produce satisfying results for troubled pastors or their denominations.

Parishioners and Pastors Falling in Love

Parishioners Falling for Pastors

Parishioners of both sexes fall in love with their pastors. The subject here is romantic love that seeks a reciprocal relationship, often sexual, with the beloved. It can arise out of pastoral counseling situations where intimate matters are discussed in sequestered sessions. When a husband and a wife in the congregation have a troubled marriage and seek counselling from their pastor, the pastor may be used as a model of comparison by the spouse of the opposite sex. That is, if the pastor is male, the wife may compare her problematic husband with the wonderful pastor and develop an emotional attachment to the pastor. It can also occur in the course of day-to-day parish activities—committee meetings, choir practice—where there is regular interaction between pastor and parishioner.

The more common scenario is female parishioners falling in love with male pastors. One reason is that denominations today have more female than male parishioners and more male than female pastors. Demographics aside, a more significant reason is that male pastors tend to show themselves as sensitive and considerate. Compared with the husband who won't talk about his feelings and spends his free time watching football or working on his car, the average male pastor seems to be a paragon of sensitivity and relational commitment.

The most widely used personality inventory in North America is the Minnesota Multiphasic Personality Inventory (MMPI). One section of the MMPI is a masculinity-femininity clinical scale, which recently has been revised to reflect changes in cultural attitudes since the 1930s. This scale was initially developed to identify homosexuality, but over the years, it has revealed something else about pastors. Male Protestant clergy have tended to score high on the femininity scale, regardless of their sexual orientation.

High interest in personal relationships and emotional sensitivity are considered feminine traits, but they characterize most pastors, male or female. They are also what women frequently say they want in a partner. Therefore, male pastors are subject to affectionate attachments from female parishioners.

More often than not, these feelings of love are not revealed explicitly to the pastor, although an intuitive pastor may pick up signals. As long as the signals are ignored, these infatuations may wane over time with no harm done. When they are openly confessed, however, pastoral wisdom is required in dealing with the parishioner. There is only one rule in how to respond when this happens: Do not reciprocate the feelings. Be kind. Be flattered. But do not encourage the infatuation. Unrequited love has a way of running its course, evolving eventually into a fondness that resides in the heart without need for reciprocation. Let it be.

Pastors Falling for Parishioners

The reverse situation occurs when pastors fall in love with parishioners. The subject here is not extramarital affairs or sexual misconduct, although either could develop from it, and both often do. Emotional affairs that involve little or no physical contact are possibilities, too, and these can be as difficult to deal with as sexual liaisons. This is dangerous territory. Any pastor who is beginning to feel romantically drawn to a parishioner should study chapter 3 of this book concerning the need for pastors to maintain emotional distance from parishioners. The rule for pastors who become infatuated with members of their congregations is: Do not say anything to the object of your affection, but do tell a therapist or spiritual director.

If for some reason a pastor does speak of love to a parishioner, and that person expresses confusion or in any way indicates the feelings are not mutual, the pastor must immediately stop the romantic quest and offer apologies for the behavior. If the person indicates similar infatuation, the problems are just beginning.

Let's assume that the pastor's intentions are honorable. We are not dealing here with a pattern of sexual conquests. Because of some personal dynamic, the pastor has developed a romantic attachment to a parishioner. How does this play out in the context of parish ministry, where the pastor is the spiritual leader?

Regardless of other circumstances, if the attachment arises in the context of pastoral counseling or pastoral care, acting on it is unwise by human standards, improper by church standards, and unethical by the standards of all the helping professions—therapists, physicians, social workers, clergy, and so on. Experiencing affectionate feelings for another person in the course of counseling is normal. Acting on the feelings is problematic, and many knowledgeable people today characterize pastors who act on these feelings as abusers.

For a pastor who is married, falling in love with a parishioner is an untenable situation. Divorce among pastors is widely accepted today, but divorce from one's spouse and remarriage to a member of the congregation being served are not. If a pastor's marriage is failing, falling in love with someone else will seriously complicate the process of dealing with the marital problems, and it will hamper any chances for continued ministry with the present congregation. It may mean the end of all future ministry for the pastor.

A single pastor who falls in love with an unmarried parishioner whose feelings are mutual may be able to survive the situation with ministry intact if the courtship leads to marriage. Even so, the pastor may have to endure the passive-aggressive wrath of other members who may have been interested in a romantic relationship with the pastor. If marriage does not occur, the pastor and parishioner are both wounded, and both may be obliged, for a variety of reasons, to leave the parish.

Either party, for example, may experience a broken heart and suffer painful reminders of the relationship each time the other is seen in church. So either may need to leave at least temporarily to avoid being hurt again. And, of course, the parishioner has lost a pastor in the process of becoming involved romantically with the pastor. A return to a normal pastor-parishioner relationship is not reasonable to expect in such circumstances. Both parties need to acknowledge this fact, and the parishioner is entitled to encouragement in seeking another pastor. Assuming the romance was known publicly, either partner may feel great embarrassment that it has come to an end, especially if the decision to break up was unilateral. This may lead to considerable gossip throughout the congregation and very likely will result in the pastor's being held in lower esteem by many in the congregation.

I know a number of pastors who married members of congregations they served, and most of these marriages have succeeded. But some have encountered unanticipated complications as a result. Commonly, either the pastors remain tied to that congregation or immediate area for an entire career because of family requirements, or they are pressured to relocate prematurely.

Generally, the younger the pastor and the parishioner, the better the congregational acceptance. Also, associate pastors in multiple staff churches are given wider latitude in dating a member of the congregation. However, the limit is one. Unmarried pastors of any age or status who become romantically involved with more than one person in a congregation (serially or otherwise) find themselves in big trouble.

Responsibility

This is a complex subject with many nuances beyond the scope of this appendix. Nevertheless, it is clear that in relationships of the heart, pastors must exercise great self-control. Regardless of who has fallen in love with whom, the pastor must take responsibility for the denouement.

NOTES

Introduction

1. This is my own translation into modern English.
2. Desiderius Erasmus, *The Praise of Folly*, 1668 English translation by John Wilson (New York: Joseph Simon, 1979), 72.
3. Ibid., 105.

Chapter 1

1. I am grateful to Dr. Jake Thiessen for introducing this idea into our weekly breakfast conversations.

Chapter 5

1. Dorothy McRae-McMahon, *Being Clergy, Staying Human: Taking Our Stand in the River* (Washington, D.C.: The Alban Institute, Inc., 1992), 5.
2. Daniel T. Hans, *God on the Witness Stand: Questions Christians Ask in Personal Tragedy* (Grand Rapids, Mich.: Baker Book House, 1987).
3. Frederick Buechner, *The Sacred Journey* (San Francisco: Harper & Row, 1982), *Now and Then* (San Francisco: Harper & Row, 1983), *Telling Secrets* (San Francisco: HarperCollins, 1991).
4. Beuchner, *Telling Secrets*, 3.

Chapter 6

1. In denominations with a pastoral search committee process at the congregational level, newly called pastors commonly experience feelings of disappointment or even betrayal when they discover that the wonderful search committee members who nominated them turn out to be unrepresentative of the congregations. Typically, search committee members are among the most committed and active members of their congregations. When pastors discover how few others out there are like them, bad feelings may occur. In such cases, the honeymoon feeling in the congregation may last longer than the honeymoon feeling in the pastor. It is unrealistic for pastors to expect search committees to be representative of their congregations, even when they say they are.

Chapter 7

1. Roy M. Oswald, *How to Build a Support System for Your Ministry* (Washington, D.C.: The Alban Institute, Inc., 1991). Roy Oswald's consulting work in Carlisle Presbytery, where I serve, forms the basis for this book.

Chapter 9

1. Each denomination has its peculiar ethos and its own pathos as well. In large ecumenical gatherings denominational personalities can be discerned as pastors talk, behave, and dress in widely varying ways. It seems likely that characteristic patterns of pathology may also emerge from different denominations. Working with several denominations to provide therapy for pastors, Jake Thiessen has noticed behavioral differences between pastors from churches with hierarchical polities and those from churches with independent polities. If pastors in certain denominations show tendencies toward particular pathologies, this information could be quite helpful to people charged with responsibility for them. More research is needed in this area.

2. To learn what strategies one tends to rely on in conflict situations, see Speed B. Leas, *Discover Your Conflict Management Style* (Washington, D.C.: The Alban Institute, Inc., 1984). This booklet includes a survey instrument, score form, and interpretive material.

Chapter 10

1. Expensive gifts from individual members are another matter.
Gifts of jewelry, personal apparel, large sums of money, or anything that
causes a pastor discomfort should be declined with as much tact and
courtesy as possible. Some parishioners seek favor or influence through
gifts much as lobbyists do with politicians. Pastors would do well to
accept graciously the box of grapefruit from Florida, the souvenir desk
ornament, or the twenty dollar bill tucked into a holiday card. But gifts
that are inappropriately intimate or immodestly expensive need to be
returned. Acceptance of a gift that seems suggestive of romantic affection will send an encouraging signal to the giver. Beware! Of course,
what constitutes an unacceptable gift is a judgment call arising out of the
social culture of the congregation and the specific dynamics of the relationship between pastor and gift-giving parishioner. When in doubt, ask
a colleague. This advice does not apply to gifts from the congregation as
a whole. Grateful congregations frequently present expensive gifts (e.g.,
checks for thousands of dollars or trips to the Holy Land) to pastors at
retirement or special anniversaries of service. When these gifts are
offered, accept them humbly.

Afterword

1. For a sobering account of this problem, see Paul Wilkes' article
"The Hands That Would Shape Our Souls," *Atlantic Monthly*, December
1990, 59-88.
2. These are my own couplets, following Chaucer's meter.

The Alban Institute:
an invitation to membership

The Alban Institute, begun in 1974, believes that the congregation is essential to the task of equipping the people of God to minister in the church and the world. A multi-denominational membership organization, the Institute provides on-site training, educational programs, consulting, research, and publishing for hundreds of churches across the country.

The Alban Institute invites you to be a member of this partnership of laity, clergy, and executives–a partnership that brings together people who are raising important questions about congregational life and people who are trying new solutions, making new discoveries, finding a new way of getting clear about the task of ministry. The Institute exists to provide you with the kinds of information and resources you need to support your ministries.

Join us now and enjoy these benefits:

CONGREGATIONS: The Alban Journal, a highly respected journal published six times a year, to keep you up to date on current issues and trends.

Inside Information, Alban's quarterly newsletter, keeps you informed about research and other happenings around Alban. Available to members only.

Publications Discounts:

☐ 15% for Individual, Retired Clergy, and Seminarian Members
☐ 25% for Congregational Members
☐ 40% for Judicatory and Seminary Executive Members

Discounts on Training and Education Events

Write our Membership Department at the address below or call us at 1-800-486-1318 or 301-718-4407 for more information about how to join The Alban Institute's growing membership, particularly about Congregational Membership in which 12 designated persons receive all benefits of membership.

 The Alban Institute, Inc.
Suite 433 North
4550 Montgomery Avenue
Bethesda, MD 20814-3341